WRITERS AND THE

ISOBEL ARMSTR
General Edit

BRYAN LOUGHREY
Advisory Editor

W. B. Yeats

W. B. YEATS

W·W

W. B. Yeats

Edward Larrissy

Northcote House
in association with the
British Council

© Copyright 1998 by Edward Larrissy

First published in 1998 by Northcote House Publishers Ltd, Plymbridge House,
Estover Road, Plymouth PL6 7PY, United Kingdom.
Tel: +44 (01752) 202368 Fax: +44 (01752) 202330.

British Library Cataloguing-in-Publication Data
A catalogue record for this book is available from the British Library

ISBN 0-7463-0830-2

Typeset by PDQ Typesetting, Newcastle-under-Lyme
Printed and bound in the United Kingdom

Contents

Preface

This book studies Yeats's work (chiefly his poetry) in the belief that it is meaningful to think of Irish writing as the product of a colonial and post-colonial society. In his case this means paying due attention to the fact of his Protestant, Anglo-Irish identity, an identity with much potential for a sense of division, especially in the case of a poet who was also committed to the cause of Irish national liberation. Yeats's interest in the occult, and the masonic connections of the Order of the Golden Dawn, are both better understood in the light of his Anglo-Irish background.

My method is broadly influenced both by a Marxian cultural criticism, and by Deconstruction. This blend of influences, which still seems paradoxical to some, has continued to constitute one of the chief tendencies in contemporary literary criticism. It underlies, for instance, the 'New Historicist' work of Marjorie Levinson on Keats and Wordsworth. It provided the basis for my study of William Blake (1985). And it is a dominant tendency in the post-colonial theory of Gayatri Spivak and Homi Bhabha. One of the most incisive exponents of the new post-colonial criticism of Irish writing, David Lloyd, acknowledges his indebtedness to Paul de Man. Premature obituaries for Deconstruction were written in the late 1980s. My impression is that, after a brief lull, the influence of Derrida is gathering pace yet again, and on a very wide front. The advantage for the cultural critic in drawing on some of the emphases of Deconstruction lies in an enhanced sensitivity to effects of deferral and difference, though these are then assigned to cultural causes – a fact which, of course, limits the sense in which such criticism can genuinely be termed 'Deconstructionist'. But a methodological discussion both broader and more detailed than this one can await my Introduction.

The analyses I offer, and the conclusions I draw, are broadly in agreement with those to be found in my longer work, *Yeats the Poet: The Measures of Difference* (Hemel Hempstead: Harvester Wheatsheaf, 1994), although there I cover topics not discussed in any detail here, such as Yeats's Orientalism, his changing relation to the Gaelic tradition, and the precise nature of certain of his occult sources. The totality of conclusions I reach has been regarded as controversial by some (though not by others). I have not, however, yet encountered any objections that are sufficiently well grounded to shake my confidence, and some of them are being quietly withdrawn. Yeats studies in Britain (though not in the USA) have for some time now been dominated by those who are well qualified to engage in disputes about whether or not Yeats was thought, because of his sallow complexion, to have 'yellow blood'. But, in estimating the true meaning of his engagement with Rosicrucianism or the Gaelic tradition, they have been hampered by the ignorance of the minute specialist and therefore by the complacency of a largely spurious semblance of rigour. While I would certainly claim to offer a theoretically grounded view which has been largely absent in Britain, the reader can also have confidence in the historical and linguistic research which provides its material.

Acknowledgements

The Collected Poems of W. B. Yeats: A New Edition (1991), edited by Richard J. Finneran, reproduces the texts to be found in *The Collected Works of W. B. Yeats*, vol. 1, *The Poems*, revised and edited by Richard J. Finneran (New York: Macmillan, 1989). Twelve lines from 'Easter, 1916' are reprinted with the permission of Simon and Schuster from this edition. Copyright © 1924 by Macmillan Publishing Company, renewed 1952 by Bertha George Yeats. Nine lines from 'Meditations in Time of Civil War' and four from 'Among School Children' are reprinted with the permission of Simon and Schuster. Copyright © 1928 by Macmillan Publishing Company, renewed 1956 by George Yeats. Permission was also given by Macmillan (UK), and by A. P. Watt Ltd., on behalf of Michael Yeats.

Biographical Outline

1865   William Butler Yeats born (13 June) in Dublin, son of John Butler Yeats and Susan (née Pollexfen).

1866   Susan Mary (Lily) Yeats born.

1867   The family moves to London.

1868   Elizabeth Corbet (Lolly) Yeats born.

1871   Jack Butler Yeats born.

1884   Yeats enters the School of Art, Dublin.

1885   Yeats a founding member of the Dublin Hermetic Society. First poems published in *Dublin University Review*.

1887   The family returns to London. Yeats joins the Blavatsky Lodge of the Theosophical Society, and publishes his first poems in English magazines.

1888   Yeats joins the esoteric section of Theosophical Society. Edits *Fairy and Folk Tales of the Irish Peasantry*.

1889   Yeats publishes first book of poems, *The Wanderings of Oisin and Other Poems*. Begins edition of Blake with Edwin Ellis. Meets and falls in love with Maud Gonne.

1890   Joins the Hermetic Order of the Golden Dawn.

1891   Founding member of the Rhymers' Club, London–Irish Literary Society, and National Literary Society in Dublin, with John O'Leary as President.

1892   *The Countess Kathleen and Various Legends and Lyrics* and *Irish Fairy Tales*.

1893   *The Celtic Twilight* (fairy and folk tradition); and *The Works of William Blake*, 3 vols. (with Edwin Ellis).

1894   Meets Mrs Olivia Shakespear.

1895   *Poems* (his first collected edition). Edits *A Book of Irish Verse*.

1896   Meets Lady Gregory. Member of the Irish Republican Brotherhood.

1897	*The Secret Rose.*
1898	Plans Irish Literary Theatre with Edward Martyn and Lady Gregory.
1899	*The Wind among the Reeds.*
1900	Yeats's mother dies. He forms a new Order of the Golden Dawn after disagreements with Aleister Crowley and MacGregor Mathers.
1902	Becomes president of the Irish National Dramatic Society. *Cathleen ni Houlihan* is performed in Dublin, with Maud Gonne in the title role.
1903	Maud Gonne marries John MacBride.
1904	*In the Seven Woods.* The Abbey Theatre, Dublin, opens. Yeats is producer-manager.
1905	*Stories of Red Hanrahan.*
1906	*Poems 1895–1905.*
1907	Yeats defies rioters at performance of J. M. Synge's *The Playboy of the Western World.* Tours Italy with Lady Gregory and her son Robert. His father departs for New York.
1908	*Collected Poems,* 8 vols. Visits Maud Gonne in Paris. Meets Ezra Pound.
1909	Death of J. M. Synge.
1910	Yeats receives a Civil List pension of £150 p.a.
1911	Meets his future wife, George Hyde-Lees.
1913	Ezra Pound acts as Yeats's secretary.
1914	*Responsibilities.*
1915	Yeats refuses a knighthood.
1916	The Easter Rising. Maud Gonne's husband, Major John MacBride, is executed for his part in it. Yeats proposes to Maud Gonne and is refused.
1917	Yeats proposes to Maud Gonne's daughter, Iseult, and is refused. Marries George Hyde-Lees (20 Oct.) Shortly afterwards she begins to produce the automatic writing which provides the material for *A Vision. The Wild Swans at Coole* and *Per Amica Silentia Lunae* published.
1919	Anne Butler Yeats born (26 Feb.) in Dublin. Move to Ballylee. Winter spent in Oxford. *The Only Jealousy of Emer.*
1920	American tour, accompanied by Mrs Yeats.
1921	Michael Butler Yeats born (22 Aug.). *Michael Robartes and the Dancer.*
1922	Irish Free State established. Irish Civil War as a result of

Constitution accepting the partition of Ireland. Yeats made a senator of the new state.

1923   Yeats receives the Nobel Prize for literature, and visits Stockholm to receive it (Dec.), where he delivers his acceptance speech, *The Bounty of Sweden*.

1924   Work towards completion of the first version of *A Vision*. Visits Sicily (Nov.).

1926   First version of *A Vision* published Jan., dated 1925.

1927   Congestion of the lungs and influenza lead to collapse.

1928   Rapallo, in N. Italy (Apr.). Declines to stand for re-election to Irish Senate because of ill-health. *The Tower*.

1929   Last visit to Ballylee in the summer. Collapse from Malt fever in Rapallo (Dec.).

1931   Receives D.Litt. from Oxford (May). Spends winter at Coole Park with Lady Gregory, who is dying.

1932   Death of Lady Gregory (May). Yeats helps to found Irish Academy of Letters.

1933   *The Winding Stair and Other Poems. Collected Poems.*

1934   A rejuvenation operation (the 'Steinach operation'). *Collected Plays.*

1935   Attacks of lung congestion. Collaborates with Shri Purohit Swami on translation of *Upanishads*. *A Full Moon in March* published.

1936   Seriously ill. Heart problems and nephritis. BBC broadcast on Modern Poetry. His edition of *The Oxford Book of Modern Verse* published. *Essays 1931–1936.*

1937   Jan.–Mar. in the south of France. Last public appearance for Abbey Theatre performance of *Purgatory* (Aug.). *New Poems*. Second version of *A Vision*.

1939   *Last Poems and Two Plays*. Dies 28 Jan. Buried Roquebrune, France.

1948   Yeats's body reinterred at Drumcliff churchyard, Sligo.

Abbreviations

Au.	*Autobiographies* (London: Macmillan, 1955; repr. 1970)
Ex.	*Explorations*, ed. Mrs W. B. Yeats (London: Macmillan, 1962)
L.	*The Letters of W. B. Yeats*, ed. Allan Wade (London: Rupert Hart-Davis, 1954)
M.	*Mythologies* (London: Macmillan, 1959)
P.	*The Collected Poems of W. B. Yeats: A New Edition*, ed. Richard J. Finneran (London: Macmillan, 1991)
VI	*A Vision: An Explanation of Life founded upon the Writings of Giraldus and upon Certain Doctrines Attributed to Kusta ben Luka* (London: privately printed, 1925)
V2	*A Vision* (London: Macmillan, 1937)
VP	*The Variorum Edition of the Poems of W. B. Yeats*, ed. Peter Allt and Russel K. Alspach (New York: Macmillan, 1957; rev. 1966)

Note on the Text

The edition of Yeats's poems used in this book is *The Collected Poems of W. B. Yeats: A New Edition*, ed. Richard J. Finneran (London and Basingstoke: Macmillan, 1991). This is the same text as *The Poems: A New Edition*, ed. Richard J. Finneran (2nd edn., London and Basingstoke: Macmillan, 1991), and the page numbers for all the poems discussed in this book are exactly the same, though it omits some of the uncollected poems and the notes on the copy-texts at the end of the latter volume. The editing of Yeats's poems to be found in these volumes is the result of the most pondered and rigorous train of thought by a scholar who is also well versed in the niceties of modern textual theory. A dispassionate assessment of its competitors is to be found in a recent work on Yeats's own construction of his books by an outstandingly incisive and original scholar, Hazard Adams, in his *The Book of Yeats's Poems* (1990). This uses Finneran's text, and accepts 'Finneran's ordering and his decisions about inclusion and exclusion, except for his placement of the longer poems' (p. 16). Of the rationale of Finneran's chief competitor, *Yeats's Poems*, edited by A. Norman Jeffares and promoted by Warwick Gould, Adams has these words to say: 'This will not do' (p. 15).

If the reader wishes conveniently to possess in one volume a generous selection of poems, plays, criticism, occult speculations, speeches, and letters, then the indispensable purchase is in The Oxford Authors series (General Editor, Frank Kermode): *W. B. Yeats: Selected Writings*, ed. Edward Larrissy (Oxford: Oxford University Press, 1997).

1

Introduction

YEATS AND THE IRISH TRADITION

'Irish poets, learn your trade,' enjoins Yeats, in one of his last poems, 'Under Ben Bulben', which is something of a last will and testament. One of the things this poem does, as befits such a testament, is to convey Yeats's own sense of where he himself belonged in the tradition of Irish poetry, as well as his sense of what was best in that tradition. But of what tradition are we speaking? Many readers outside Ireland, especially in Britain, possess only the vaguest notion of what an Irish poetic tradition might be, if indeed they realize that such a thing exists at all. This last point of ignorance is less common in the USA and Europe, where there is often a tendency to romanticize Ireland and her mysterious Celtic past, even where there is little detailed knowledge. But in Britain, ignorance fed by prejudice can still permit a columnist in *The Times*, supposedly a paper for educated people, to deride the notion that there could be anything of value in the study of the Irish language, dismissing it as fit for nothing more subtle than pub discussions of racing form and the scores of hurling matches.

Yeats did not know Irish, and his efforts to acquire it met with as little success as his efforts to acquire other languages. He avowed that, though Irish was his national language, English was his mother tongue. Yet it is central to a true understanding of Yeats, and of other writers of the so-called Irish Revival, that there had grown up, since the early Middle Ages, an extensive, rich, and various literature in Irish, comprising – among other genres – epic sagas, romances, and lyric poems. Some of these writings are transcriptions of oral traditions with their roots in the pre-Christian Iron Age. A vital part of the inspiration of

1

Yeats, J. M. Synge, and Lady Gregory is bound up with the idea of *revival* in a fairly precise sense: the revival, albeit in the English language, of a power, a pathos, and a corpus of myths and legends, which had once found embodiment in the Irish-language tradition. For many people of Yeats's background (he came from the Protestant middle class), the idea that such a tradition had existed was almost as new and outlandish as it is to many modern English people. Matthew Arnold, in his lectures on *The Study of Celtic Literature* (published in 1867), had informed his Oxford audience, with pedagogic zeal, that 'Of Irish literature, the stock, printed and manuscript, is truly vast.' But this information was not well known. Instructively, the formative moment in the literary career of the Irish antiquarian Standish James O'Grady (1846–1928) was the wet afternoon when, inhibited from his customary sports, he repaired to the library of an Irish country house and took down some books of Irish history. He stayed, with increasing wonder and amazement that the ancestors of people, many of whom his caste regarded as little better than savages, had once possessed a distinctive and by no means contemptible culture.

There was something of the excitement of rediscovery, then, in the Irish Revival. Of course, Yeats grew up in the cultivated environment fostered by his artist father, and came to know people who knew something about Irish tradition during his student years in Dublin. In any case, the antiquarian, scholarly, and literary rescue of the Gaelic past was not something that suddenly began in the 1890s. Scholarship in Irish language and antiquities had never been completely extinguished, and the Romantic period had given new impetus to rediscovery, with translations and commentaries such as those to be found in Charlotte Brooke's *Reliques of Ancient Irish Poetry* (1789) or James Hardiman's *Irish Minstrelsy* (1831). Furthermore, there were translations and reworkings of real literary distinction to be found in the works of the poets James Clarence Mangan and Sir Samuel Ferguson, both of whom Yeats admired and regarded as forerunners of the Revival. Ferguson, in particular, saw it as his task to convey the power and sophistication of some of the best Irish poetry through the medium of nineteenth-century English poetic convention, and many would agree with Yeats that he achieved considerable success in this ambition. Yeats also read the antiquarian works of scholars such as Eugene O'Curry, and the articles and translations to be found in the *Transactions* of the Ossianic Society, which was based in Dublin.

The title of this society, 'Ossianic', points conveniently to an important related topic: the exotic charm of things Celtic in the nineteenth century. The adjective is formed from the name 'Ossian', and makes direct reference to the prose poems published by James Macpherson in the 1760s, which are sometimes referred to simply as *Ossian*, or *The Poems of Ossian*. This publication is not exactly the first moment in the gradual ascent of the Celt, among readers, to special status as a combination of natural poet and noble savage: arguably, that honour belongs to William Collins's 'Ode on the Popular Superstitions of the Scottish Highlands'. But it is a decisive moment. The celebrity of *Ossian* in Europe – it was translated into most of the European languages, and admired by Goethe, Chateaubriand, and Pushkin – created a climate of feeling in which even those who doubted its genuineness sought to offer something more authentically Ossianic. Among the latter were Irish antiquarians, incensed that the Scots were claiming credit for the legends of Oisin (*osheen*). Even in the Outer Hebrides, the ballads of Oisin frequently evoked an Irish setting, and made clear reference to the famous Irish hero, Fionn mac Cumhail, whose son he was.

The later history of Celticism on a European stage includes Ernest Renan's *Poetry of the Celtic Races* and Wagner's *Tristan und Isolde*. In America, Walt Whitman never doubted the authenticity of Macpherson's efforts. In the British Isles, Arnold not only fostered the notion of the poetic Celt, but also helped to develop the image of noble defeat which became something of a cliché. Arnold had quoted a line from Macpherson which had helped to foster this image: 'They went forth to the battle, but they always fell.' Yeats chose this as the initial title of the poem which later became 'The Rose of Battle'. The Celtic peoples, defeated and marginalized in the wars of this world, could nevertheless sing angelically and with all the apparent ineffectuality of Shelley. By the 1890s, the aesthetic movement encouraged some artists to think of Celtic art as providing models for a future age which would transcend the barbarous materialism of the nineteenth century, and a poet such as Yeats's friend Lionel Johnson

(1867–1902) could feel that it was valuable to emphasize his Irish connections on the basis that he was of Irish descent. Yeats's first major poem, *The Wanderings of Oisin* (1889) (*P.* 355–86), can in part be understood in the context I have outlined: its subject is Ossianic, being a version of the most celebrated tale associated with the legendary poet Oisin about how he was enticed away to a land without death by a beautiful woman of Faery called Niamh. It could thus be seen as quintessentially Celtic, and, by the time it was published, this was becoming a quality of great fascination to many metropolitan as well as Irish readers.

THE ANGLO-IRISH ASCENDANCY

The Irish Revival was overwhelmingly brought about by the talents and exertions of authors who came from a group of people as prolific in literary accomplishments as any in Europe have ever been – namely, Anglo-Irish Protestants. From this caste had come, in the eighteenth century, Edmund Burke and the philosopher Berkeley. One of the two greatest nationalist politicians of the nineteenth century, Charles Stewart Parnell, was an Anglo-Irish Protestant. And in the Revival, J. M. Synge, Sean O'Casey (born John Casey), Lady Gregory, Douglas Hyde, and George Moore were all Protestants. In a later generation, Samuel Beckett was a Dublin Protestant. Yeats was brought up as a communicant of the Anglican Church of Ireland, like most (though not all) of the Irish middle and upper classes of his day. His father (John Butler Yeats, 1839–1922) was an artist who had trained for the Bar, his mother (Susan *née* Pollexfen, 1841–1900) came of a Sligo shipowning family. Those who were descended at least partly from English stock, and were Church of Ireland in religion – and their ancestors might include Catholics who had converted to Protestantism – were known by the inexact but useful term 'Anglo-Irish'. The forebears of many of them had profited by the confiscation of property from Catholics, especially in the Cromwellian period and after the Treaty of Limerick (1691), which sealed the victory of the Protestant William of Orange over the forces supporting the Catholic James II. During the eighteenth century their power had been buttressed by a battery of penal laws imposing disabilities

4

upon Catholics: restricting their access to education, limiting their property rights, demanding tithes to Protestant clergymen. Considered as a ruling class, the Anglo-Irish were called the 'Ascendancy'. But this term describes a structure of relative power and influence only, and can disguise a variety of conditions if taken too literally. An Anglo-Irish person might be a humble clerk, a small farmer, or a Church of Ireland parson (as was Yeats's grandfather at Drumcliff, Co. Sligo); nor were all Catholics indigent peasants. Yeats's family, scarcely aristocrats in any case, were, as he grew up, constantly on the edge of financial catastrophe, through the uncertainty of his father's employment as an artist and portrait-painter.

The resulting insecurity may be one of the reasons for Yeats's growing espousal, from his middle years onwards, of aristocracy. But the insecurity should also be seen as endemic to the Anglo-Irish caste. There are some who object to the word 'colonial' as applied to the Irish condition during Yeats's early life (and to the word 'post-colonial' as applied to that condition today). And one can well understand an objection which claims that this word is capable of eliding a history of quite extraordinary complexity. But once one has conceded that no two histories, and no two colonies, are alike, it is hard to think of a better example of a colonial polity than eighteenth- and nineteenth-century Ireland, with its various repressions of a caste of more or less dispossessed helots, many of whom, in the earlier part of the period, resentfully remembered a time when either they, or lords they could at least identify with as members of a common culture, had been in possession of the land, speaking a language different from that of the new Ascendancy, wearing different clothes, observing different customs, remembering different lore, and practising a different religion. The resistance that members of this caste were prepared to offer at periods of crisis encompassed violence and danger of death, imprisonment, or transportation: that is always the acid test of the way a subaltern class experiences its conditions.

The insecurities of colonial identity breed narratives of anxiety, but also of compensation, and this was notably true of the hyphenated Anglo-Irish identity. The work of Samuel Ferguson provides some notable examples of anxiety. His 'Dialogue between the Head and the Heart of an Irish

Protestant' bears witness to a conflict between a deracinated impulse towards Irish patriotism, on the one hand, and sectarian suspicion and prejudice, on the other. His poem 'Mesgedra' displaces the colonial predicament onto ancient Irish saga material:

> For thou, for them, alas! nor History has
>   Nor even Tradition; and the Man aspires
> To link his present with his Country's past,
>   And live anew in knowledge of his sires;
>
> No rootless colonist of an alien earth,
>   Proud but of patient lungs and pliant limb,
> A stranger in the land that gave him birth,
>   The land a stranger to itself and him.

It was early enough indeed when the Protestant Bishop Ussher, in the seventeenth century, proposed that the Church of Ireland, rather than the Catholic Church, was the true descendant of the Celtic Church of St Patrick, and this particular way of pretending to be more Irish than the Gaels remained in evidence right up until Yeats's day. It is also fair to say that many of the best scholars of Irish antiquities in the nineteenth century were Anglo-Irish, and they could feel that they had played no mean part in preserving and translating the relics of the Celtic past – perhaps a less biased part than was likely to be played by Catholic priests. And, however much one might wish to insist that the Anglo-Irish had by Yeats's time earned the right to be regarded as Irish, some of the energy of the Irish Revival comes from a congenital sense of distance from the Catholic peasantry, especially from those whose folk tradition still retained something of the ancient pagan Celtic beliefs, and whose immemorial practices of storytelling and recitation seemed to make them living embodiments of the image of Celt as poet. To try to obscure this distance, which was the result of old and bitter conflicts, is simply to make many of the characteristic products of the Revival harder to understand. For instance, J. M. Synge, the son of a wealthy and strongly anti-Catholic landowning family, reveals this distance in the combination of idealization and mockery one finds in his work. At the heart of this is the idea of the Irish peasant as naturally poetic, as the Preface to *The Playboy of the Western World* (1907) makes clear. And although that

6

is a comedy which is unsparing in its revelation of Irish fecklessness and folly, his journal, *The Aran Islands*, and his tragic play, *Riders to the Sea* (1904), reveal the Gaelic west as the homeland of people who possess an almost mystical innocence and intensity. Both the idealization and the mockery are the product of a distance for which the Gael is, by turns, exotic primitive and priest-ridden serf.

It would not be entirely accurate to equate Yeats's experience of the Irish peasantry with that of Synge. During his youthful sojourns in Sligo he acquired a familiarity with the ordinary local people which Synge never possessed at the same age. Nevertheless, he retained the mark of the contrast between life in London, on the one hand, and the Sligo world of folk tale and superstition, on the other. It is the simple truth to say that Yeats became a considerable amateur folklorist, whose collections of stories, gathered by himself or others, were published in book form in *Fairy and Folk Tales of the Irish Peasantry* (1888), *Irish Fairy Tales* (1892), and *The Celtic Twilight* (1893). These living remnants incited his first interest in Celtic tradition, only gradually supplemented by a scholarly interest in Irish mythology and the ancient literature, starting, of course, with *Oisin*.

Yet he himself is a good example of the characteristic Anglo-Irish sense of division. His work is full of juxtapositions of contrary states ('The Song of the Happy Shepherd' (P. 7–8) next to 'The Sad Shepherd' (P. 8–9)) or dialogues between opposed aspects of the self ('Self' and 'Soul', or 'Hic' and 'Ille'): compare Ferguson's 'Head and Heart' of an Irish Protestant. While it would be difficult to decode these examples directly in terms of Irish conflicts, it is easy to believe that an innately Irish division is their ultimate source. A reading of the *Autobiographies* supports such a view, with a vivid evocation of the young Anglo-Irish boy, moving between Sligo and London, fully at home in neither world. Interestingly, this last phrase could be applied to Oisin in *The Wanderings*. Oisin stays with Niamh for 300 years as mortals count them. Yet, while there, he comes to yearn for the vigorous reality and companionship he has lost. In the end he rides back over the waves, intending a short visit, but with the warning that, if his foot touches the ground, he will age by all the years that have passed in an instant, and he will not be able to return to Niamh. When he arrives in Ireland, he stoops to

7

help two men carrying a sack, and his foot touches the ground. He discovers that, in the intervening years, Ireland has become Christian, and he conducts a vigorous debate with St Patrick, defending the values of his own era of pagan heroes against what he sees as the puny morality of Christianity.

It will readily be seen that the poem does not provide an exact equivalent between the opposition of England and Ireland, for it employs three terms, rather than two: pagan Ireland, the Islands of the Immortals, and Christian Ireland. It is Christian Ireland that most corresponds to a category that, in late Romantic fashion, Yeats normally affects to despise – what he calls 'Grey Truth' in 'The Song of the Happy Shepherd', associating it there with the modern or post-pagan world. To be explicit about all three places: pre-modern, pagan Ireland can be seen as a displaced image of an idealized Ireland – those aspects of it that still believe in Faery and at the same time value heroism and combativeness; the Islands of the Immortals are representations of the poet's 'dreams' (as Yeats was inclined to call them); and Christian Ireland is, in part, a displaced image of the modern world, of which England is the most awful example. Simply to treat these displacements as equations would be absurdly reductionist. But, as we shall see, there is much in Yeats's work that supports a reading which includes these terms.

The terms can be figured as a triad, with Fenian Ireland (that is, the Ireland of Fionn and his warriors) at the centre. To the one side is the world of imagination, which elicits desire, but may lead one away from earthly happiness. To the other side is the world of truth and duty, which represents a threat to imagination. At the centre is a world in touch with either side, a world that encounters imagination, but does not simply retreat into it; a world that values reality, but not the abstractions that some would make out of it. Oisin was a poet and harper, and his world is a world fit for the ideal poet: one who tempers dream with the praise of reality, and who knows that a good song needs a 'measure'. This is not a world to which the priestly guardians of Catholic Ireland can lead us, any more than can St Patrick. That task, it may be suggested, belongs to the Anglo-Irish poet, as other evidence confirms.

It will be seen that I have suggested that the Anglo-Irish poet can mediate between Celtic imaginativeness and the abstractions of a world of 'Grey Truth'. There are a number of passages in his *Autobiographies* which offer more direct and explicit support for this suggestion. Thus, in *Reveries over Childhood and Youth* (1914) Yeats thinks of the fineness that might emerge if he could impose the 'right image' on the 'soft wax' of the Irish condition:

> O'Leary had once said to me, 'Neither Ireland nor England knows the good from the bad in any art, but Ireland unlike England does not hate the good when it is pointed out to her.' I began to plot and scheme how one might seal with the right image the soft wax before it began to harden. I had noticed that Irish Catholics among whom had been born so many political martyrs had not the good taste, the household courtesy and decency of the Protestant Ireland I had known, yet Protestant Ireland seemed to think of nothing but getting on in the world. I thought we might bring the halves together if we had a national literature that made Ireland beautiful in the memory, and yet had been freed from provincialism by an exacting criticism, a European pose.   (*Au.* 101–2)

It falls to the Anglo-Irish poet to blend cosmopolitan premeditation and Celtic impulse. But at the same time, the poet may come to notice and find value in contrasting ways of life and philosophies. It was in the occult tradition that Yeats found some of the symbols and terminology to convey the value of being able to see the truth in both sides of an opposition. Or, to employ Yeats's habitual usage, the truth in 'antinomies' – that is, opposing or contrary principles.

OCCULTISM, FREEMASONRY, AND IRISH GOTHIC

'Without contraries is no Progression,' asserts William Blake in *The Marriage of Heaven and Hell*. This is a work Yeats would have known exceedingly well, for he could be described as one of the first true scholars of Blake. The three-volume edition of Blake's works with commentary (1893) that he edited with his friend Edwin Ellis is the first attempt at a full and serious edition, and even includes black-and-white reproductions of many of the engraved plates. Yeats would also have been well aware of Blake's sources in the occult tradition. Blake's phrase about contraries is nearly a direct quotation from Jakob Boehme, the

9

mystical writer, whose thought was moulded by philosophical alchemy: that is to say, by the tradition of interpreting alchemical symbols in terms of their spiritual significance. (It is a tradition which, as it happens, had a considerable influence on the psychology of C. G. Jung.) The general tendency of philosophical alchemy is to interpret the philosopher's stone (by which gold could be made) as a spiritual rebirth achieved by the integration of the opposed principles symbolized by mercury and sulphur, the fundamental substances of the alchemist's art. The opposed principles were masculine and feminine, and could also be symbolized by sun and moon, fire and water, even (in a seeming contradiction) by gold and silver. An obvious reference in Yeats to this body of symbolism is to be found at the end of 'The Song of Wandering Aengus' (P. 59–60), where the speaker, finding his ideal feminine counterpart, and thus integration of the masculine and feminine poles of the psyche, will 'pluck till time and times are done | The silver apples of the moon, | The golden apples of the sun'.

But Yeats was not merely a theoretician of magic, he was also a practitioner. To be blunt, he was a magician. This means that when we read, for instance, his essay on 'Magic' (collected in *Essays and Introductions*) we are not to think of it as embodying the speculations of a scholar, but rather the conclusions of an adept, whose knowledge was acquired in the magical order known as the Hermetic Order of the Golden Dawn, which Yeats joined in 1890. The most important members of this included Samuel MacGregor Mathers, Aleister Crowley (later notorious as a practitioner of 'Sex Magick'), A. E. Waite (the designer of a Tarot pack still current, and author of a history of Rosicrucianism), and the real founder, the Revd. William Wynn Westcott (author of a book on the seventeenth-century Rosicrucian, Robert Fludd). The doctrines of Rosicrucianism (a synthesis of occult and philosophical traditions, including Neoplatonism and the Kabbalah) were supposedly founded upon the teachings of the legendary Christian Rosenkreutz. As refined by Fludd, whose influence on Rosicrucianism in the British Isles was decisive, these doctrines developed into a synthesis of Neoplatonism, Kabbalah (Jewish mystical writings), Christology, astrology, and alchemy. They also comprised theories of ritual invocation and geomancy (divination by the manipulation of earth or sand). Yeats's membership of the inner orders of the Golden Dawn, his use of the symbols of Rose and Cross (an early notebook is entitled 'The Rosy Cross Lyrics') and his composition of the poem 'The Mountain Tomb' (*P.* 121–2) (refrain: 'Our Father Rosicross is in his tomb') make it clear that he thought of himself as a Rosicrucian, at least during the years of his membership.[1]

This fact has an unexpected resonance for those who are familiar with the history of Rosicrucianism, for in nineteenth-century Britain and Ireland this history is intimately interwoven with that of Freemasonry. It was normal for Masonic lodges to include inner orders of speculative masons whose interests were in the occult sciences in general, and in their Rosicrucian synthesis in particular. The piquant fact is that Freemasonry in Ireland was a pervasive institution of the Protestant Ascendancy. A good example of such a person is provided by Yeats's uncle, George Pollexfen, a Freemason and adept of astrological lore. But in any case, a little research will show just how pervasive among the Anglo-Irish that institution was. Oscar Wilde himself was a Freemason, and was raised to the Apollo Rose-Croix (Rose-Cross) Chapter of the Apollo Lodge in Oxford.

The point of noting these facts is not to raise an eyebrow at the depth of Yeats's Protestant inheritance, though the information is interesting; rather it is to find enlightenment in the obviously non-Catholic character of Freemasonry in Ireland, and then to see how this helps to shed light on the attraction of the Golden Dawn for Yeats. For the magic of the Golden Dawn offered a means of access to supernatural wonder, and an authority over it, that could more than vie with the Catholic Church, and, moreover, allowed individual creativity. Furthermore, by what at first seems a paradox, Yeats could think of himself not only as a magician but as a Druid, and this brought him nearer to, rather than further from, the Celtic spirit of Ireland. The doctrines of Freemasonry and of Rosicrucianism were often thought to originate in the near East, in Egypt or Israel. But so were those of Druidism. The Irish antiquarian, Eugene O'Curry, described Druidism as 'that form of the Eastern Philosophy or Religion which prevailed in early ages in our own as well as other western nations'.[2] Another scholar whom Yeats read asserts that 'the Irish druids were magicians, neither more nor less'.[3] Yeats tended to think in terms of universal archetypes, and that would be sufficient to allow that all magicians discovered the same truths. But he had the added support of scholars who thought that Druidism had originated in the Orient.

The contemporary conception of the druids' functions sheds a reflexive light on the way the Golden Dawn magician saw himself. Yeats's friend, the scholar and translator Douglas Hyde, notes that the druid 'was looked upon as an intermediary between man and the invisible powers'.[4] This makes another triad, with the Golden Dawn druid in the middle, mediating between the supernatural and the mundane. This structure helps to make it clearer that, as R. F. Foster puts it in his important Chatterton Lecture of 1989, the 'Anglo-Irish occultist' might exercise a unifying and mediating role.[5]

UNITY

Unifying might seem an attractive enterprise to one who was conscious of a divided inheritance. The conscious striving for unity is strong in Yeats. 'Hammer your thoughts into unity' is a phrase he repeated to himself as a young man. 'Unity of Being' was an ideal he proposed for himself. And, contemplating the Irish nation, he longed to encourage Unity of Culture. One aspect of this drive to unity which people do not always remember is the extent to which Yeats sought to unify the individual and the social by giving a public shape to his inner convictions and inspirations. Where others might have been satisfied to read about magic, Yeats joined an order of magicians. Where others might have been satisfied to try and give Ireland a dramatic literature by writing plays, Yeats had to help found a new national theatre and then help to run it. And where others sympathized with the cause of Irish national liberation, Yeats joined the Irish Republican Brotherhood (another secret society), which had a tradition of violent separatism, though this was fairly moribund by the 1890s. Furthermore, Yeats saw all these different areas, and more, as interrelated. The most important point to take from this is that joining two such different secret societies was part of one large enterprise in Yeats's mind. The freedom of Ireland must be sought. But it must accompany a new flowering of its ancient imaginative temperament. That temperament included the belief in supernatural powers; and the modern druid of the Golden Dawn might assist in discovering their nature. As for his poetry, that could serve the idea of Ireland's liberation, and it could take as its subject ancient myths and legends and magical occurrences and beings. Indeed, Yeats was conscious that the use of Irish myth and legend permitted the exploitation of a range of material not yet wearied with overuse, as he felt that classical myth was. But this is still to relegate the influence of myth and magic to a fairly superficial level. For Yeats in a sense thought that poetry was magic. Like all magicians he thought that words and invocations and chanting and symbols had the potential to summon up supernatural powers. The difference from poetry was only that the latter was less systematic in its magical practice. When reading an essay such as 'The Symbolism of Poetry' (originally published in the same volume as the essay on 'Magic') one needs to be aware that Yeats intends literally the formulations which suggest that the symbols of poetry call down supernatural powers.

The poem which best illustrates this unity of purpose in the early Yeats is, fittingly enough, a kind of manifesto, and it is one that is both artistic and political: 'To Ireland in the Coming Times' (P. 50–1), at the end of the series called *The Rose*. First, he states the poetic tradition to which he belongs: he wishes to be accounted one of a company 'That sang, to sweeten Ireland's wrong'. Later in the poem he names some of the poets he has in mind: 'Davis, Mangan, Ferguson'. An important motive of Yeats appears to be the desire to quell doubts about whether he is indeed a truly patriotic poet:

> Nor be I any less of them [the company],
> Because the red-rose-bordered hem
> Of her whose history began
> Before God made the angelic clan,
> Trails all about the written page.

She is Eternal Beauty, whose symbol is the Rose, and the least we can deduce from this is that Yeats is rebutting the argument that his poetry is too aesthetically inclined to have any political effect. But, remembering that some of the connotations of the

Rose are occult ones, we might also suspect that he is answering the objection that occultism can have no political effect, either. This view is supported by what follows, for in the second stanza he asserts that he should not be regarded as less of a patriotic poet because 'the elemental creatures go | About my table to and fro, | That hurry from unmeasured mind'. As mage he is constantly able to summon spirits emanating from the eternal mind, but this is in no sense an unpatriotic activity, as the apostrophe at the end of the stanza makes clear: 'Ah, faeries, dancing under the moon, | A Druid land, a Druid tune!' The spirits are the 'faeries', who still converse with the Irish folk of his day, and who were once worshipped as gods in pagan Ireland. Their priesthood was the institution of Druidism, resuscitated by the Order of the Golden Dawn. True freedom for Ireland lies in a confident reassertion of the ancient Celtic spirit, of which vital traces are still to be found in its folk memory. These were beliefs which Yeats never relinquished for long. As he says in 'Under Ben Bulben', which I have described as his last will and testament, 'And ancient Ireland knew it all.'

2

Early Yeats:
The Rose of Ireland

THE UNITY OF THE ROSE

Yeats devised a scheme for the earliest lyrics he wished to preserve whereby, among other things, he would embody the effect of unity achieved out of difference by means of some of his favoured symbols, particularly that of the rose. In *Poems* (1895), he grouped together some early lyrics under the heading *Crossways*, and some other lyrics from *The Countess Kathleen and Various Legends and Lyrics* (1892) under the heading *The Rose*. In Hiberno-English, the word 'crossways' can be a synonym for 'crosswise', i.e. 'in the shape of a cross'. It can also refer to small roads or pathways crossing a larger thoroughfare. The reference to the cross is strengthened by the deliberate juxtaposition with another series called *The Rose*, for we know that Rose and Cross are the chief symbols of Rosicrucianism. The Rosicrucians believed that the cross of Christ should be equated with the Tree of Life, the chief symbol of the Jewish mystical writings in the Kabbalah, which, in accordance with an established Renaissance trend, they subjected to a Christian interpretation. The Tree of Life stretched into the very abode of God, and the adepts of the Golden Dawn believed that it was possible to ascend it, through various states of being, by means of magical invocations and visualizations. In doing so, they would travel along 'pathways'. An important theme introduced in *Crossways* is that of the wandering spirit of life, with which one should be in sympathy. As it says at the end of 'Ephemera' (*P.* 15), 'our souls | Are love and a continual farewell'. In 'The Madness of King Goll' (*P.* 16–18), the ancient Irish king who is the speaker seems to have been driven mad by an oversensitivity to the variety and force of experience, and wanders around registering this condition:

> And I must wander wood and hill
> Through summer's heat and winter's cold,
> *They will not hush, the leaves a-flutter round me, the beech leaves old.*

The poems in *Crossways* are quite various in style and subject matter, as befits the idea of various states of being. They include ballads (e.g. 'The Ballad of Father O'Hart'(*P.* 21–2)), a version of an Irish folk song ('Down by the Salley Gardens' (*P.* 20–1)), a brief verse drama on an Indian subject ('Anashuya and Vijaya' (*P.* 10–13)), two other Indian poems, a treatment of a legendary ancient Irish subject ('The Madness of King Goll' (*P.* 16–18)), a poem about the fairies kidnapping a child ('The Stolen Child' (*P.* 18–19)), and the two 'contrary' shepherd poems ('The Song of the Happy Shepherd' and 'The Sad Shepherd').

Mention of contraries leads us conveniently to consideration of a growing emphasis in Yeats criticism, one that has relevance to the titles and construction of *Crossways* and *The Rose*. As long ago as 1955 Hugh Kenner pointed out that the care with which Yeats constructed his books indicated that he wished to fulfil the symbolist project of constructing a 'sacred book', 'The Sacred Book of the Arts', where design, typeface, and especially the positioning of poems, both in relation to their neighbours and in terms of the whole book, would convey meaning with the optimum of power and intensity.[1] More recently, Hazard Adams has built on this insight by emphasizing the element of contrariety and conflict encouraged by the placing of poems and books.[2] This emphasis is consonant with the juxtaposition of poems taking contrary views, as in the shepherd poems, but it also addresses the relationship between books. Thus, *The Tower* (1928) is followed by a book which goes inside the tower, *The Winding Stair and Other Poems* (1933). The former book was associated with assertiveness, bitterness, and violence, the latter with a quality of sweetness which Yeats thought of as more inward, ruminative, and feminine. So with the groups known as *Crossways* and *The Rose*. Where the former emphasizes variety and contrariety, the latter tends more to unity, as befits the image of a rose.

16

The Rose is indeed the chief image of unity in Yeats's early work. It is a compound image, which expresses unity achieved out of many different strands of thought and feeling. It can be identified as a rose that grows out of the centre of the mystical Tree of Life. It is also more specifically the Rose of Rosicrucianism, which represented a feminine principle, in *The Rose* identified by Yeats with the eternal beauty the male poet seeks. More specifically still, it is the woman he loves, Maud Gonne. But it is also another feminine figure: Ireland, so often in the Irish poetic tradition personified as a woman, young or old. Yeats's play, *Cathleen ni Houlihan* (1902), gives an account of the arrival of a mysterious old woman in a cottage in the West of Ireland at the time of the French invasion attempt in the 1790s. She represents the spirit of Ireland, often personified as Cathleen ni Houlihan, or as the Poor Old Woman. In the penal age there grew up a tradition of patriotic poetry in which a beautiful woman, who looks like one of the fairies or *sidhe*, is encountered in a vision. These poems were known as *aisling* ('vision') poems. But the woman did not have to be a vision. One of the best-known personification poems is the folk song 'Mo Róisín Dubh' ('My Little Dark Rose'), in which the speaker comforts the weeping Róisín (namely, Ireland) and looks forward hopefully to Spanish intervention (the poem probably originated in the seventeenth century). Apart from being frequently sung, it became famous among the lettered in a rather free translation by James Clarence Mangan, 'My Dark Rosaleen'.

The Rose series, unlike the *Crossways* one, is for the most part characterized by a lofty homogeneity of style, and by a concentration on Irish subjects, mythical and legendary. All this fits with the achievement of a unity of the kind outlined above. The series betrays evidence of judicious positioning of poems, and this is evident from the first poem, 'To the Rose upon the Rood of Time', which balances the last, 'To Ireland in the Coming Times', which I have already described as a kind of manifesto. 'To the Rose' is more like a statement of intent, but, like 'To Ireland', it makes the link between the patriotic and the occultist strands in the poetry fairly clear. An invocation of the Rose at the beginning of the poem is intended to enlist aid so that the poet can sing of 'the ancient ways'. By this, he goes on to assert, he means that he intends to sing of the ancient saga

17

material of Ulster: of the warrior-champion Cuchulain, and of the druid who showed Fergus, king of Ulster, the forms of existence of all things, leaving him sad with too much knowledge. The connection with occult thought is made clear when he returns to his general ambitions, and speaks of finding 'under the boughs of love and hate, | In all poor foolish things that live a day,| Eternal beauty wandering on her way'. The boughs of love and hate are the contraries or antinomies of the Tree of Life as it reveals itself in this world, for this is not a world where unity comes naturally. More simply, they are a metaphor for the sheer contrariety of this world in all its multiplicity, which is why we find 'all poor foolish things that live a day' under the boughs. But what we find within them, as their principle, is 'Eternal Beauty'. The Rose that grows out of the centre of the conflict-ridden Tree of Life – thus appropriately identified with the Cross, or Rood – is to be found not far beneath the appearances of this various and conflictual world.

That world is appropriately referred to by the juxtaposition later in the series of 'The Rose of Peace' (P. 36) and 'The Rose of Battle' (P. 36–7). But the most extended image of the multiplicity of this world is to be found in 'Fergus and the Druid' (P. 32–3), which develops the theme of the transmigration of souls. (The druids were widely held to have believed in this, and Yeats's later interest in reincarnation should be seen in that light.) Fergus has looked into the druid's 'bag of dreams' which contains images of all the modes of life in this world:

> I have been many things –
> A green drop in the surge, a gleam of light
> Upon a sword, a fir-tree on a hill,
> An old slave grinding at a heavy quern,
> A king sitting upon a chair of gold –
> And all these things were wonderful and great;
> But now I have grown nothing, knowing all.
> Ah! Druid, Druid, how great webs of sorrow
> Lay hidden in the small slate-coloured thing!

This is Yeats's version of a paradox familiar from Browning: try to seek knowledge of all things, and you will be left with nothing; on the other hand, throw yourself with sufficient vigour into your own particular mode of life, and you will find everything in that way. Fergus takes the former route; but, again like some self-maiming character from Browning, he already seems to lack sufficient vigour and confidence, since he wishes to resign the kingship.

The Rose is also the heart, and having confidence in one's own heart is an important prescription of early Yeats. This theme is brought in relation to the Tree of Life image in another poem in *The Rose* series, 'The Two Trees' (*P.* 48–9), which begins: 'Beloved, gaze in thine own heart, | The holy tree is growing there.' The second of the two stanzas is scarcely so joyful (two contraries within one poem): 'Gaze no more in the bitter glass' of the 'demons', for there 'a fatal image grows': 'Roots half hidden under snows, | Broken boughs and blackened leaves.' The glass should not be seen as the mirror of vanity, but more simply in its role as reflector: it is secondary, rather than original: it does not come from the heart. Therefore it shows a dead tree. The occult source upon which Yeats is drawing here is the Kabbalah of Isaac Luria, known as the Lurianic Kabbalah, which describes a myth of the Fall in terms of which the divine light departs from the Tree of Life, leaving it as a dead husk or outline of bark. The spheres of existence also become 'husks'. Interestingly, the Hebrew word used for 'husks' in this context, *Qlippoth*, also means 'demons'.

There is no suggestion at this point that the Tree has become dead for Yeats. Rather, the message seems to be that his own heart is at one with the occult, passionate, and Irish matter he has synthesized. Indeed, the message is in part circular, for at the same time the occult and Irish matter tell one to have confidence in one's own heart and to make a unity of experience in relation to its promptings. This confident tone has to a large degree evaporated by the end of the 1890s.

THE SONG OF WANDERING AENGUS

Before considering the melancholy tone which makes its way into some of the lyrics in the important volume *The Wind among the Reeds* (1899), it will be worthwhile examining in some detail one of the most successful poems of Yeats's early period, 'The Song of Wandering Aengus', as this will serve to bring together some of the themes both of the introduction and of this chapter.

This has been well called an *aisling* or vision poem, though it is not of the kind already described, since the woman is not a personification of Ireland – not, at any rate, a direct personification. Aengus, or Aengus Óg (young Aengus), or the Mac Óc (the young son), is one of the former gods of Ireland, described by Yeats as the god of love. The poem illustrates the appropriateness of that description.

His going out to the hazel wood and cutting a hazel wand have a magical meaning, not only because of the word 'wand', but also because hazel is a magical wood in Celtic tradition. We should already suspect, then, that when he goes fishing with this wand, the formless fire of masculine desire in his head will be met by something magical. It scarcely hinders matters that this magical fishing takes place at the twilight before dawn, and hard by a stream: for here we have two boundaries, one temporal and the other spatial. Temporal and spatial boundaries are magical in Celtic and other traditions, because they are supposed not to be actually within space or time. They therefore represent as it were a crack in nature through which the supernatural may intervene. He catches a little silver trout but, not inappropriately, the trout turns into a girl, for the element of water is feminine. We should immediately realize that this is one of the *sidhe*, the fairies. She now turns the tables on him: '[She] called me by my name and ran | And faded through the brightening air.' She already knows his name, and her calling is a choosing full of magical power. When she runs, he cannot choose but follow, 'Through hollow lands and hilly lands' – that is, through the contraries of earthly existence. He believes that he will find her in an immortal land which seems like Tír na nÓg ('The Land of the Young', where live the undying *sidhe*), for we can deduce that it is full of apple orchards, which grew there, as they probably did in the British Avalon. And there they will both together 'pluck till time and times are done | The silver apples of the moon, | The golden apples of the sun'. To achieve a true marriage (which is what this mystical joining of archetypal contraries implies) is also in a sense to be the master of time; to control and to enjoy the fruits of the two aspects of time, night and day, and their traditionally appropriate functions, intuition and reason.

Technically the poem distils a superbly deft concentration of meaning and suggestion. All goes to enhance the uncertainty of twilight. The white moths and the 'moth-like stars' intensify the impression made by each other. Not only are the stars 'flickering', but the girl is 'glimmering', and soon the air is 'brightening'. This impression of visual variegation is supported by an auditory one: something 'rustled' on the floor. When, in the third stanza, the happy land is discovered, the flickering light of the orchards is described ('long dappled grass') so that it is as if the first event finds fruition in the last. The impression of a sunny orchard is intensified by the internal rhyme of 'dappled' and 'apples'. In fact, the poem, like the collection from which it comes, is a symbolist masterpiece. But it also remains entirely to the point that, as we have seen already, Yeats did not think of the symbolism of poetry in isolation from the symbolism of magic: it is not just that the poem is about magic, but that it is also meant to evoke in our minds the universal archetypes of human love, which Yeats believed to have a real spiritual existence. This should be remembered in a reading of his essay, 'The Symbolism of Poetry'.

A consideration of metrics will also provide instruction. No enjambement affects the tetrameter line, and the poem has a simple lyric movement of some intensity. (This last quality is also procured by the number of lines strung together with the conjunction 'And': not a metrical effect, of course, but one should always assess the interaction of metre with other elements in the poem.) The employment of the metre itself is entirely orthodox, with the exception of the odd extra unstressed syllable in words such as 'flickering' and 'glimmering'. Of course, the fact that it is these words that profit by the extra syllable is itself another factor tending to emphasize both their presence in the poem and their likeness to each other.

This orthodoxy is shared by other poems of Yeats, including those which Yeats himself suggested were characterized by 'faint and nervous' rhythms, or by 'wavering' rhythms. Some readers have tended to take Yeats's assessment too far, and assume that there is something radically innovative about the versification of some early books, particularly of *The Wind among the Reeds*. Adelyn Dougherty's *A Study of Rhythmic Structure in the Verse of William Butler Yeats* (1973) was undertaken for the Mouton Press, which specializes in advanced literary theory

21

and stylistics, including metrics. She found that Yeats's work, early and late, was characterized by a marked adherence to the norms of English metrics, except for a tendency to add or omit the occasional extra unstressed syllable, as in 'Song of the Wandering Aengus', where some are added. The effect of wavering uncertainty might be brought about by the combination of this kind of loosening with other characteristics of the poem, especially a long line, as in 'The Valley of the Black Pig' (P. 65–6). While Yeats's ideal of musicality in verse undoubtedly derives from the notion of Celtic poetry as notably musical, his practice bears no relation whatsoever to the complicated metrics of Gaelic poetry. The point is this: Yeats's practice of versification is entirely consonant with the ideal of the Anglo-Irish poet writing in English measures, into which he introduces just sufficient of a quality of looseness and indefiniteness to suggest the supposed Celtic love of the infinite.

THE WIND AMONG THE REEDS

The excellence of *The Wind among the Reeds* (1899), possibly the one true symbolist masterpiece in the English language, has for long been obscured by the anti-Romantic battles of early twentieth-century Modernism. The fact that early Yeats is now increasingly the subject of study and appreciation has much to do with the powerful and detailed readings to be found in Harold Bloom's *Yeats* (1970), who studies the dynamic relationship between Yeats's poetry and that of the Romantics and Victorians. On a simple historical note, it should be remembered that Yeats was born only thirty-eight years after the death of his admired William Blake. It is hardly surprising that his work is influenced not only by Romantic but also by Victorian poets, including of course the pre-Raphaelites. A knowledge of Romantic and Victorian poetry can be an advantage in making more precise one's sense of what a poem by Yeats is attempting to achieve. By the time he comes to composing most of the poems which end up in *The Wind among the Reeds*, Yeats has also been able to profit from some acquaintance with the theories and the practice of French symbolism, in particular through the expert knowledge of his friend Arthur Symons, author of *The*

Symbolist Movement in Literature. Paul Verlaine's cry of 'De la musique avant toute chose' ('Music before everything') in 'Art Poétique', and Mallarmé's plea for the employment of suggestion, have left their mark on the distilled power of a poem such as 'Song of the Wandering Aengus'.

The Wind among the Reeds has been the subject of a very probing and scholarly book by Allan Grossman which studies the characteristic interaction in it of occult and ancient Irish images.[3] And this combination should serve to remind us that the book represents an intensification not just of imagery, symbolism, and verbal music, but also of Irish nationalist hopes. The titles we have now, many of them beginning with 'He' or 'The Lover' (as in 'The Lover mourns for the Loss of Love' (P. 61) or 'He remembers forgotten Beauty' (P. 62–3)), are revisions of the titles in the first versions and in the first edition, which usually specify a named speaker. Some of these names are those of ancient Irish heroes, as in 'Aedh laments the Loss of Love' (first edition), Aedh being a companion of Fionn mac Cumhail. Another is, significantly, the name of a Jacobite poet of the penal era who wrote in Irish: 'O'Sullivan Rua to Mary Lavell' is the first published version of 'He remembers forgotten Beauty' (*Savoy*, July 1896). Eoghan Ruadh Ó Súilleabháin (Owen Rua or Roe O'Sullivan) composed, among other fine lyrics, the *aisling* poem 'Ag Taisdiol na Bláirne' ('Strolling through Blarney'), in which the poet encounters the usual beautiful and unhappy woman, Ireland. Yeats's reference is unambiguously political. Furthermore, some of the nationalist sentiments in the volume take on an apocalyptic aspect. This seems appropriate enough to a volume published in the very year of *fin de siècle*, 1899. We are not, of course, surprised to be informed that, despite the date, 'Your mother Eire is always young' (P. 59). But, despite all that we have learnt of Yeats's espousal of national liberation, we may be surprised to encounter the vision described in 'The Valley of the Black Pig':

> unknown spears
> Suddenly hurtle before my dream-awakened eyes,
> And then the clash of fallen horsemen and the cries
> Of unknown perishing armies beat about my ears.

We may be surprised, that is, if we read Yeats's own explanatory note (P. 455), which begins 'All over Ireland there are prophecies of the coming rout of the enemies of Ireland, in a certain Valley of the Black Pig.' Yeats is seldom so explicit about his nationalist hopes.

Nor is he usually even in this volume. The general context is the need for a profound renewal of the Irish spirit. Although in 'Into the Twilight' (P. 59) he speaks of the eternal youth of mother Eire, he makes it clear that he is speaking in 'a time out-worn'. And the poem is addressed to his own 'Out-worn heart'. Personal renewal and political renewal are presented as connected needs. At the personal level, the chief problem is that he is irrevocably separated from his beloved, the chosen partner of his soul:

> Knowing one, out of all things, alone, that his head
> May not lie on the breast nor his lips on the hair
> Of the woman that he loves until he dies.

There will be no plucking and eating of golden and silver apples for him. That would represent the desired integration and renewal of the self. Ireland also requires such renewal, which will not only be political in the narrow institutional sense, but will entail the return to Celtic sensibility. It does not take much imagination to see that throwing off British domination will not be enough; the stifling repression of the Catholic Church will have to go as well.

The mood of despair is encapsulated in a poem which ended the first edition, and is now last but one, 'He thinks of his Past Greatness when a Part of the Constellations of Heaven' (P. 73). The first point to consider is the change of title. In the first edition it was 'Mongan thinks of his Past Greatness'. Mongan was a medieval king who was taken to be a reincarnation of the hero Fionn mac Cumhail. The greatness for which he laments is thus the past greatness of heroic Ireland. The poem begins by informing us that he has 'drunk ale from the Country of the Young' (Tír na nÓg, the land of the fairies) and weeps 'because I know all things now'. We have already seen from 'Fergus and the Druid' that knowing all things can be a disabling possession. And Mongan has learnt all things in the same way as Fergus: he has actually been all things, has been through all transmigrations in the quaffing of an ale. He provides a brief list:

> I have been a hazel-tree, and they hung
> The Pilot Star and the Crooked Plough

> Among my leaves in times out of mind:
> I became a rush that horses tread:
> I became a man, a hater of the wind...

We know that a hazel tree is magical. The Pilot Star (the pole star) and the Plough (probably the constellation of Ursa Major, even though Ursa Minor is nearer to the pole star) could only be among the leaves of a very tall tree. Here we have the Tree of Life again, identified with the Celtic hazel tree, with the world revolving around it, just as it revolves around the pole star. Furthermore, the tree even has an affinity with Irish nationalism, for the Starry Plough is a traditional nationalist emblem (compare Sean O'Casey's *The Plough and the Stars*). The principle of life is bound to have an affinity with any movement that will liberate the Celtic spirit. That Mongan has been Fionn mac Cumhail is one measure of his decline. But he has also been another great man; for the revised title of the poem, about having been part of the constellations, is a reference to Blake's Albion. In the address 'To the Jews' at the beginning of Chapter 2 of his long poem *Jerusalem*, Blake informs them that they had a tradition that man used to contain all things: 'this you received from the Druids. | "But now the Starry Heavens are fled from the mighty limbs of Albion."' The totality of associations means that the Celtic spirit has fallen from mystical identity with the cosmos, probably in the pagan age of Fionn mac Cumhail. Reference to Fionn might itself be understood politically, however, since the name of his warrior band, the *Fianna*, was the source of the English word 'Fenians', and this term, in self-consciously heroic fashion, was used for the members of the Irish Republican Brotherhood – of whom Yeats was one.

From Tree of Life to rush that horses tread is a swift and demeaning descent. Equally to the point, it is one that refers to the title of the volume, *The Wind among the Reeds*. That title makes reference to the tradition of the Aeolian Harp, a loosely strung instrument, of some vogue in the Romantic period, which was left where the wind might touch it so that it would make natural music, responding to the wind of life, as in Coleridge's poem 'The Eolian Harp'. The idea had already been given a Celtic twist by Macpherson, who has Ossian hang his harp up in a tree, where it makes mournful music. And as long ago as medieval Ireland the image might be transferred to vegetation, so that the woods themselves became the harp, the tree branches the strings. This is also the conceit to be found in Shelley's 'Ode to the West Wind': 'Make me thy lyre, even as the forest is.' The title of Yeats's volume suggests that the robust music of Fenian Ireland has descended to a mournful, reedy sound. As for the speaker of this poem, he is a 'hater of the wind', the wind of life which has ensured that he will never be with the woman he loves.

An apocalypse must be a time of destruction as well as new creation, and *The Wind among the Reeds* leaves it open to us to remember this as we read it. Yet the hints of melancholy and disillusionment are deep and disturbing. Yeats sometimes hits a note where grief and depression are strikingly combined, as in the closing lines of 'He mourns for the Change that has come upon Him and his Beloved, and longs for the End of the World' (*P.* 61–2):

> I would that the Boar without bristles had come from the West
> And had rooted the sun and moon and stars out of the sky
> And lay in the darkness, grunting, and turning to his rest.

This is the same Black Pig that was supposed to presage the liberation of Ireland. But in this poem the apocalypse is total, and it is what the speaker longs for. The vicissitudes of Yeats's relationship with Maud Gonne have much to do with the depressed mood of some of these poems, especially perhaps that of 'He thinks of his Past Greatness' (*P.* 73), the composition of which postdates her revelation that she had had a lover for many years. Disillusionment with the course of this relationship is one of the precipitating factors in Yeats's development of a new and, as he would see it, harder style in the opening years of the new century. But it would be a pity to reduce to the biographical level a change of such consequence for poetry in the English-speaking world. Other factors include Yeats's reading of Nietzsche, the general sense of living in new times, and later his friendship with Ezra Pound. Furthermore, there is a piquant political correlative of the change, the full bearing of which is not often sufficiently grasped. While it has frequently been observed that Yeats becomes enamoured of the aristocratic idea, and that he finds a new respect for the traditions of the Ascendancy, it has not always been realized how strong a note of reserve about Irish nationalism enters into his thinking.

3

Mask, Image, and Aristocracy

THE MASKS OF DIFFERENCE

One of the best-known poems in *The Wind among the Reeds*, 'He wishes for the Cloths of Heaven' (*P*. 73), makes very explicit the conscious link in Yeats's early work between love and poetic creation. This is the poem in which Yeats claims that, had he 'the heavens' embroidered cloths', he would spread them under his lover's feet: 'But I, being poor, have only my dreams; | I have spread my dreams under your feet; | Tread softly because you tread upon my dreams.' By the time he had completed *Responsibilities* (1914), he felt that it would be a significant gesture to end the volume with 'The Coat' (*P*. 127), in conscious repudiation of the earlier poem:

> I made my song a coat
> Covered with embroideries
> Out of old mythologies
> From heel to throat;
> But the fools caught it,
> Wore it in the world's eyes
> As though they'd wrought it.
> Song, let them take it,
> For there's more enterprise
> In walking naked.

We can infer that the poem is not just about love's disillusionment, but also about the abandonment of the late Romantic manner, first in point of subject matter (no more old mythologies), and second in point of the adoption of a new style for which the word 'naked' is an appropriate epithet. The tone of disillusionment should be

27

noted not just for itself, but for the way it is congruent with a disillusionment with former political affiliations, which we shall have to note. And, finally, there is a disillusionment with the idealization of the beloved woman, which actually brings with it a new theory of woman which becomes bound up with some new theories about poetic creativity.

To take first the topic of woman's nature and the new theory of poetry. The most cogent introduction to this topic may be provided by a poem which, conveniently, seems to run on lines of thought parallel to those to be found in 'A Coat', though it comes from the earlier collection *In the Seven Woods* (1904). The poem is 'Never give all the Heart' (*P.* 79), in which Yeats begins by asserting that, if a man does give his heart, 'passionate' women will hardly find love worth thinking of: certainty will destroy the adventure. For they have 'given their hearts up to the play. | And who could play it well enough | If deaf and dumb and blind with love?' In this poem, at any rate, woman's nature dictates that the lover, to be successful, give his 'heart' up to 'the play'. What seems unified and essential – the heart – must be expressed in the deferral and role-playing for which Yeats finds a metaphor in drama, in the pondered insincerity for which he develops a term derived from the theatre: the mask. So the repudiation of a certain idealistic view of love also entails a reversal of values: it will be recalled that in 'The Two Trees' Yeats had asserted that there is no truth except in one's own heart, and that one should avoid the secondariness and externality of the dead tree in the mirror. Furthermore, a knowledge of the Kabbalistic sources of that poem revealed that the dead tree was associated with the bark or husk of the living tree. But now we find Yeats rejecting the heart and choosing the mask, which has overtones of externality as well as of insincerity.

In the same volume, connected thoughts are to be found in 'Adam's Curse' (*P.* 80–1), where Yeats speaks of the minute and arduous labour of writing poetry as 'stitching and unstitching'. The comparison with 'women's work' is deliberate, for the woman to whom he is talking in the poem goes on to observe that women understand that 'we must labour to be beautiful'. The labour of self-presentation – the mask – is part of the curse of the fall, as Yeats goes on to assert: 'It's certain there is no fine thing | Since Adam's fall but needs much labouring.' This descent into the world of time and death – the world of difference and conflict – parallels the giving-up of the heart to the play, and, like that, is the result of women's enticement. The evidence points to a significant implication: Yeats is concurring in the tradition that Adam's fall is the result of Eve's tempting him. The prescription for the male poet is to beat woman at her own game of masks and deferral, but not, of course, by adopting a feminine mask. There is sufficient evidence to show that he thought of the new style he adopted in the early years of the twentieth century as more 'masculine'. Thus, in a letter to George Russell ('AE') in 1904 he says that he finds in his own early verse 'an exaggeration of sentiment and sentimental beauty which I have come to think unmanly....I have been fighting the prevailing decadence for years...it is sentiment and sentimental sadness, a womanish introspection....Let us have no emotions...in which there is not an athletic joy' (L. 434–5).

That love is characterized by the pursuit of images rather than the essential heart or soul of the beloved is strongly confirmed by the dramatic poem, *The Shadowy Waters* (P. 403–32). In this, the sailor-poet Forgael has managed to acquire the harp of Aengus, god of love, and uses it to cast enchantment. His search for his true love is for one who will be 'the world's core' – that is to say, the world's heart (P. 416, 419). When his crew attack another ship, they kidnap the heroine, Dectora, and kill her husband. Nevertheless, she cannot help but succumb to the harp, and falls in love with Forgael, at first because she imagines him to be a hero called 'golden-armed Iollan' who died a thousand years ago. When Forgael explains that he is not Iollan, she rejoinders:

> What do I care
> Now that my body has begun to dream,
> And you have grown to be a burning sod
> In the imagination and intellect?

> (P. 427)

The metonymy of desire replaces identity. We do not find truth, or the heart, or 'the world's core' in love. As the newly enlightened Forgael explains to his companions:

> There is not one among you that made love
> By any other means. You call it passion,
> Consideration, generosity,

29

> But it was all deceit, and flattery
> To win a woman in her own despite...
>
> (*P.* 426)

Turning now to the matter of Yeats's new style, we may note that, like the lover, to win an audience a poet may employ the lies of art. Yeats's new hardness and directness of manner is rhetorical, sometimes blunt, normally a trifle exalted. Of course, it reflects the influence of his endeavours as a playwright and dramatic poet. In an essay in the drama review *Samhain* in 1904 (these essays are collected in the volume *Explorations*), he speaks of two kinds of poetry, one that paints pictures, the other that is essentially dramatic: 'In Ireland, where the tide of life is rising, we turn, not to picture-making, but to the imagination of personality – to drama, gesture' (*Ex.* 163). Furthermore, there is a versatility in the employment of different registers within the poem. Robin Skelton puts it this way in his *Celtic Contraries*:

> Yeats deliberately played literary and anti-literary, rhetorical and vulgar, ways of speech off against one another. The result was often a poem that seemed to be spoken by a man who was at once an aristocrat and a peasant, a high priest and the man next door, a man, in other words, capable of many viewpoints, many perspectives.[1]

It is a good point, though I think it overemphasizes the heterogeneity of register in Yeats's work. Nevertheless, it is a point that helps to establish more clearly that Yeats's mature style, distinctive and unmistakable as it is, achieves unity out of difference. R. B. Kershner adopts a reading that is parallel in implication, indebted as it is to the theories of Bakhtin, with their valuing of heteroglossia. He further makes the distinct but valuable point that reading Yeats is like listening to 'a speaker who uses the artifice of rhetoric... in ways that continually frustrate a reader's desire for syntactic logic'.[2] And Joseph Adams, in his *Yeats and the Masks of Syntax*, finds that Yeats's poems cultivate an undecidability which he sees as belonging to the realm of 'difference': the syntax may offer two or more meanings simultaneously, at any given stage in the poem, even though the rhetoric may enact a similarity to articulate and organized argumentation.[3]

My own example of this effect comes from a poem in *The Green Helmet and Other Poems* (1910), 'The Fascination of What's

Difficult' (P. 93). The poet begins by complaining that, in the pursuit of the difficult tasks with which he is fascinated, he has lost 'Spontaneous joy and natural content'. He goes on to register a complaint about his own personal Pegasus, steed of inspiration. Inspiration does not come easily:

> There's something ails our colt
> That must, as if it had not holy blood
> Nor on Olympus leaped from cloud to cloud
> Shiver under the lash, strain, sweat and jolt
> As though it dragged road metal.

This is not the same complaint with which the poem began, although it looks superficially similar. The first complaint was about the *fascination* of difficulty. The second is about the laborious character of his inspiration, which *makes* things difficult, although this does not now appear especially fascinating. The next complaint is about the time-consuming character of theatre business. But again, this seems to be of a different kind, on the lines of 'All things can tempt me from this craft of verse' (P. 97): not so much the fascination of what's difficult, as being too busy to get on with the fascination at all. Finally, Yeats cries out: 'I swear before the dawn comes round again | I'll find the stable and pull out the bolt.' Poetry writing, unlike theatre business, is a solitary activity ('before the dawn'). But we may be puzzled: how will it really help to find the stable? Earlier on, it was the horse itself that was the problem, not the inability to visit it. This poem is not untypical of the way in which Yeats is so concerned to create the mask of eloquence that he is ready to forgo the sinews of logic.

MORAL AND POLITICAL IMAGES

Yeats would have to wait a few years before he was able clearly to formulate a link between the theory of the mask and the belief that desire pursues images. But the political and ethical links with the theory of images are forged by the time he comes to write *Responsibilities* (1914). The epigraphs (P. 100) to this volume, when rightly understood, provide very direct instruction in those links. Thus, 'In dreams begins responsibility', said to come from an 'old play', informs us that morality is learnt by imitating ideal images ('in dreams') of rectitude, probably in other people either known, imagined, or read about. The next epigraph quotes 'Khoung-Fou-Tseu' (Confucius) as saying: 'How am I fallen from myself, for a long time now | I have not seen the Prince of Chang in my dreams.' Confucius, whose identity is founded on an idea of rectitude, cannot be that identity unless he is able to measure it against the image of probity represented by the Prince of Chang. The case with morality, then, is parallel with that of love: we both love and pursue right action in relation to images. *Responsibilities* is chiefly about right action, and it unveils Yeats's images of rectitude. There are some surprising reversals here, too.

The introductory rhymes (*P.* 101), in Confucian spirit, are an address to his ancestors, the last lines of which are an apology to them for having no child. Thus he breaks an unspoken contract with them, whereby he accepts a responsibility to continue their tradition. And who are they? A Dublin merchant, an old country scholar, and soldiers who resisted, by the Boyne, 'James and his Irish when the Dutchman crossed.' James and 'his Irish'? This is to make the identification with his Protestant ancestry specifically a matter of being Anglo-Irish rather than 'Irish'. It really is an unexpected reversal in a poet some of whose early rhymes were put in the mouth of the Jacobite poet 'O'Sullivan Rua', 'Jacobite' being the term used for those who continued to support the cause of James (Latin '*Jacobus*') after his defeat. And there are a number of other poems in the volume which express an aristocratic hauteur about certain representatives of the Catholic Irishry. 'To a Wealthy Man' (*P.* 107) is an address to Hugh Lane, who had promised to give a collection of impressionist paintings to the Dublin Municipal Gallery with some of the funds to house them, if a subscription could also be raised among the Dublin populace. The response was less than enthusiastic, but Yeats's disgust fastens on the stupidity of asking the people what they thought about art in the first place:

> You gave, but will not give again
> Until enough of Paudeen's pence
> By Biddy's halfpennies have lain...

If anything, Paudeen (Paddy) and Biddy (Bridget), whose names are supposed to be typical of lower-class Irish people, require instruction. Their opinions should not be consulted, any more than a Renaissance duke would consult the 'onion-sellers' in the market place. The implied praise for aristocratic munificence should indeed be noted. But so should the contemptuous reference to Paudeen and Biddy.

Paudeen appears again as an unpleasant old shopkeeper ('the fumbling wits, the obscure spite' ('Paudeen' (P. 109)). His mentality was no doubt behind the outraged reaction, which Yeats reviles, to Synge's *The Playboy of the Western World* ('On Those that hated "The Playboy of the Western World"' (P. 111)). And the great Protestant nationalist, Charles Stewart Parnell, is praised in terms that make Hugh Lane seem like a noble descendant of his. One of Hugh Lane's opponents in the gallery scheme had also been foremost in the rout of those who agitated against Parnell when his adultery was revealed. This is William Michael Murphy, a Catholic industrialist and newspaper owner, referred to in the poem as 'an old foul mouth'.

The target in this volume is the philistine materialism of the Catholic middle and lower middle classes. It is a quality that is not only endangering Ireland's cultural future but is removing both point and energy from the national struggle. All this becomes very plain in 'September 1913' (P. 108), where Paudeen is present in all but name:

> What need you, being come to sense,
> But fumble in a greasy till
> And add the halfpence to the pence
> And prayer to shivering prayer, until
> You have dried the marrow from the bone;
> For men were born to pray and save:
> Romantic Ireland's dead and gone,
> It's with O'Leary in the grave.

The old Fenian leader John O'Leary had been one of the younger Yeats's mentors in the 1890s. But, despite a mention of 'the wild geese' (the Gaelic aristocracy exiled in the seventeenth century), Yeats goes out of his way to stress the Protestant contribution to the national liberation struggle, mentioning Edward Fitzgerald, Robert Emmet, and Theobald Wolfe Tone. The implication is marked: Irish national liberation that will be true to Ireland's ancient spirit is not safe in the hands of the Catholic bourgeoisie. Because it has fallen into those hands,

Ireland appears to be forgetting about her national destiny. And, indeed, Yeats's poem is written in the context of increased Irish prosperity, combined with the triumph of moderate constitutionalism among nationalists.

The next volume but one, *Michael Robartes and the Dancer* (1921), contained a notable tribute to his surprise that the Easter Rising of 1916 should have come about in such a context. Although one of the elements in the surprise was that some of the chief actors in this struggle came from the Catholic middle classes of whose courage he had despaired, the people of whom he speaks in the poem cannot be summed up as coming from this background.[4] Rather, the chief content of this surprise related to issues that Yeats had already laid out years ago in what I have called his manifesto, 'To Ireland in the Coming Times'. 'Easter 1916' (*P.* 180–2) reveals combatants who in one way or another had lost contact with the soul of Ireland (to which Yeats had felt he could forge links by means of poetry and magic) and descended into the arid sloganizing and abstraction of political controversy.

It is surprising how many readers still regard this poem as a eulogy. Yet not only the outlines but the details also of Yeats's argument are abundantly clear. The outlines are these: 'I never thought much of them (in case you should be interested, here are my reasons) but they have been changed by their sacrifice.' The details encompass a beginning which shows Yeats remembering his very ordinary encounters with the future martyrs in Dublin (a town where you could 'know everybody'). On such occasions he had thought of 'a mocking tale or a gibe', and though he includes himself in the mundane comedy he imagines they live in ('Being certain that they and I | But lived where motley is worn'), he goes on to be very explicit about the reasons for mockery, in a list of some of the chief insurgents and their characteristics.

Of the Countess Markievicz, whom Yeats had known as a young unmarried woman (Constance Gore-Booth) in his Sligo days, he offers an unsparing thumbnail sketch:

> That woman's days were spent
> In ignorant good-will,
> Her nights in argument
> Until her voice grew shrill.

She had had a beautiful voice when, 'young and beautiful', she went hunting in the West of Ireland. She has succeeded in destroying her own beauty along with her good sense. (This is a good example of Yeats's growing tendency to define woman's role and capacity so as to exclude complex ratiocination.) It does not appear that Yeats was much concerned at how the Countess would feel about his opinions (she escaped the firing squad on account of her sex), since, three poems on, he supplements the sketch in 'On a Political Prisoner' (P. 183): 'Her thought some popular enmity: | Blind and leader of the blind | Drinking the foul ditch where they lie'.

The list in 'Easter 1916' continues with Patrick Pearse, a schoolmaster who 'rode our wingèd horse' – unlike the Countess, who was born to ride a real one. But the self-conscious diction verges on mockery, with the implication that Pearse was an inferior poet. Next comes another poet, Thomas MacDonagh, whom Yeats admired and liked; but the line 'He might have won fame in the end' at least toys with the thought that this is an example of wasted promise. Finally, John MacBride, Maud Gonne's separated husband, is unlikely to elicit praise; nor does he receive any. Yeats remarks that he had 'dreamed' him 'A drunken, vainglorious lout', but neglects to assert expressly that he has awoken from this dream.

'Yet I number him in the song,' is what Yeats actually writes. Grammatically speaking, this is a concessive clause, and the poem as a whole is a highly portentous concession. But, before making clear exactly what the character of the concession is, Yeats goes on to attempt to summarize his essential misgivings about the insurgents.

'Hearts with one purpose alone | Through summer and winter seem | Enchanted to a stone.' This singleness of purpose is the antithesis of the Yeatsian wisdom of being open to various points of view even to the extent of entertaining contrary positions. The clue to the meaning of the stony heart is to be found in the remarks about Con Markievicz: the pursuit of opinion and propaganda alienates and petrifies the heart. This chain of thought is confirmed by his claim in *The Death of Synge* (*Au.* 504) that 'Women . . . give all to an opinion as if it were some terrible stone doll.' The passage about the stone in 'the living stream' is superbly modulated and delicately realized, through balance, antithesis, and repetition, enacting the movement of time at the level of nature's quiet and unobtrusive beauty:

> The horse that comes from the road,
> The rider, the birds that range
> From cloud to tumbling cloud,
> Minute by minute they change;
> A shadow of cloud on the stream
> Changes minute by minute;
> A horse-hoof slides on the brim,
> And a horse plashes within it...

But still, 'the stone's in the midst of all'. The point of evoking this delicate beauty at such length is to convey both what these political agitators have renounced, and at the same time something of the endurance required by their calling.

Delicate beauty they neither possessed nor understood. Yet in one movement they have acquired 'terrible beauty'. This reference to the sublime, with its echoes of Burke's 'Terror' and Blake's 'fearful symmetry', is a measure of how far they have transcended Yeats's original definition. In one bound they have progressed from being less than fully human, to being almost superhuman. Indeed, they have become images: sublime images for an emerging nation. Just as in morality one consults images of right conduct, rather than abstract precepts, so nations ponder the images of heroes who have founded them and built their traditions. Indeed, by moving from being tediously narrow politicians to blood-stained martyrs, the insurgents have made the most effective political move of their lives. Furthermore, the poem reveals that the damage they inflicted on their own lives was part of a sacrifice, the end of which was martyrdom. In retrospect, the narrowness of their political existences was a necessary preparation. For Yeats, everyone ambitious of any achievement must sacrifice some potential. Life is too various for success on all fronts. To think otherwise is to wish, like Fergus, to 'know all' within the space of a brief, particular life. The artist and the intellectual have to make sacrifices too: 'The intellect of man is forced to choose | Perfection of the life, or of the work' (P. 246). Yeats is, in effect, offering the highest praise he knows: the insurgents have had to make a tragic bargain with destiny in the attempt to achieve their aim, and the artist has to do the same thing.

The phrase 'terrible beauty' reveals to whom they have been sacrificed. Its immediate source is the Irish writer of Gothic fiction Sheridan Le Fanu's long poem, *Duan na Glave*, which is about a Munster goddess called Fionuala: 'Fionuala the Cruel, the brightest, the worst, | With a terrible beauty the vision accurst...'.[5] As Carmel Jordan remarks, 'Like Cathleen Ni Houlihan, she demands the ultimate sacrifice of her devotees, and Cathair, a young hero like Cuchulain, gladly accepts death for her sake...'.[6] In other words, Yeats was thinking of Ireland as a terrible goddess accepting sacrifice in her cause. Furthermore, the sacrifice itself is described in Gothic terms. Nina Auerbach, in *Woman and the Demon*, notes how in *Dracula* 'The word "change", sometimes modified by "strange" and "terrible", almost always accompanies Lucy in the text...'.[7] When the insurgents exceeded Yeats's belittling definitions of them, they introduced an element of power and unpredictability, instinct with the possibility of heroism and violence. Whether or not 'England' would 'keep faith' and, as promised, reintroduce the Home Rule Bill at the end of the First World War, Yeats salutes this power, and, though he does not say so in this poem, it is a fair inference that he suspects that the insurgents have tipped the balance decisively, so that in the end it will not matter what England thinks. The point is made explicit in 'The Rose Tree' (*P.* 183): 'There's nothing but our own red blood | Can make a right Rose Tree'. Yeats not only respected blood and heroism on ideological grounds, but simply recognized them as potent forces. In all of this, he does not forget his role as national poet: 'I write it out in a verse.' Nations need their images: national bards provide them.

One must not, of course, forget the way in which this poem is founded upon a concession: on the one hand, they were mistaken, but still, and even because of their mistake, they were heroes. If the praise ends up by predominating over the criticism, this poem remains entirely congruent with the romantic and aristocratic organicism Yeats was now espousing, a position which was also associated with a renewed sense of the value of the Anglo-Irish Protestant tradition. This rarefied position is the real source of the somewhat equivocating tone of 'Easter 1916'.

VERSIONS OF ARISTOCRACY

When Yeats began to espouse the aristocratic ideal, he also began to accept what he felt that entailed. It will be recalled that, in his introductory rhymes for *Responsibilities*, he had felt the need to apologize for the fact that he had not yet fathered children. This apology is consonant with an increasing emphasis on the value of rootedness and tradition, within the context of a view of society which assumes that aristocracy is the best and most natural social development. Not only is aristocracy an organic development in itself, but it possesses an invaluable role in the organic nurturing of the best in society as a whole. When Yeats laughs at the idea of consulting Paudeen and Biddy for their views on art, he reminds us not only that Renaissance princes would never dream of doing such a thing, but that they poured their wealth into encouraging 'turbulent Italy' to delight in art and learning 'By sucking at the dugs of Greece' (*P.* 107). An aristocratic society offers models of excellence for their own sake and for the improvement of a nation over generations, because it thinks in terms of genera-tions, family, and traditions, rather than of the momentary gratification of the individual. This social conception is linked to the theory of images. In effect, society works over a considerable time to perfect an image of itself.

Yeats's conception of the aristocratic ideal is, however, subject to a radical contradiction, as Terry Eagleton has shown in a lecture delivered to the Yeats Summer School in 1985: on the one hand, there is the idea of an 'impersonal organic hierarchy to which the individual subject is – precisely – subjected'; but, on the other hand, Yeats is also drawn to the idea of the aristocrat as 'a swaggering, anarchic, Byronic affirmation of the individual subject as autonomous and absolute'.[8] This conflict is to be seen not only as between poem and poem, but also within individual poems. Such a poem is 'In Memory of Major Robert Gregory' (*P.* 132–5), which commemorates the death of Lady Gregory's son in the First World War. Yeats and his new wife, Georgie, are almost settled in their new house in the West of Ireland, Ballylee Castle. In having married and then occupied a castle, albeit a small one, Yeats has been influenced by his own notions of aristocracy. Gregory would have helped them to settle in and have ratified Yeats's almost sonship to Lady Gregory. He would also have facilitated a close and organic relationship with the land, the landscape, and the people: 'For all things the delighted eye now sees | Were loved by him.' He had time for little things like the movement of the water-hen (unlike the political agitators who got involved in the Easter Rising), but he also went hunting. And finally, he was a painter: 'We dreamed that a great painter had been born | To cold Clare rock and Galway rock and thorn.' This is the aristocrat as settled and cultivated, in accordance with the organic ideal. But there is something odd about the lines in which Yeats seeks to find the significance surrounding his death:

> Some burn damp faggots, others may consume
> The entire combustible world in one small room
> As though dried straw, and if we turn about
> The bare chimney is gone black out
> Because the work had finished in that flare.

The first few lines depict Gregory as some kind of furious genius. In other words, Gregory is now presented as more akin to the individualist notion of the aristocrat. The last line quietly introduces a new thought – namely, that Gregory has finished 'the work'. But there is simply no evidence offered in the poem – or by the facts – that Gregory could meaningfully be said to have finished some great body of work. These lines – which admittedly are merely odd, rather than outlandish – barely conceal Yeats's mixed feelings about Gregory's going to war in the first place. Gregory is, in fact, the 'Irish Airman' of the familiar anthology piece 'An Irish Airman foresees his Death' (P. 135), a poem which denies all rational justification to Gregory's enlistment:

> My country is Kiltartan Cross,
> My countrymen Kiltartan's poor,
> No likely end could bring them loss
> Or leave them happier than before.
> Nor law, nor duty bade me fight,
> Nor public men, nor cheering crowds,
> A lonely impulse of delight
> Drove to this tumult in the clouds...

Yeats's true feelings can be gauged from another poem he wrote about Gregory's enlistment, 'Reprisals', which he chose not to have published in his lifetime. In this, he bluntly accuses Gregory of gross irresponsibility in going to war and deserting his tenants – that is, of not behaving like the settled, paternalist aristocrat.

These mixed feelings derive from the fact that Gregory's 'irresponsibility' reminds Yeats that he himself has adopted a settled mode of life of whose virtues, characteristically, he is not entirely certain. Within a few poems of 'In Memory', we have 'The Collar-bone of a Hare' (P. 136–7), in which the speaker dreams of finding the collar-bone of a hare, piercing it and staring through it 'At the old bitter world where they marry in churches' and laughing 'At all who marry in churches'.

This contradiction between organicism, on the one hand, and the assertively autonomous aristocrat poet, on the other, has more than merely thematic resonance in Yeats's work. It is linked both with his characteristic style, and with some of his most idiosyncratic thinking about the image. To take first the question of style, this has been considered in a highly original reading by Cairns Craig, who points to the fact that, although Yeats is known for his belief in eternal images in the Great Mind, many of his most important poems are marked by the cultivation of associations which proffer themselves as the momentary responses of a mind very much of this world.[9] 'In Memory of Major Robert Gregory' might provide a case in point. It is structured around what are supposed to be the momentary recollections of the speaker: 'Lionel Johnson comes the first to mind'; 'And then I think of George Pollexfen'. Appropriately enough, the last stanza informs us that he had intended a different poem, one that recalled all his heroes; but 'a thought of that late death' had diverted him.

The poem also suggests a related point: when Yeats recalls Gregory's relationship with the landscape, the assumption is that he had learnt to love all its particularity, and had done so because of the growth of beloved associations. The general idea of the value of an organic and durable relationship with a particular country and people is in part predicated on the notion, often to be found in a type of conservatism now largely defunct, that ties of affection are built up by association. Craig notes that there had always been an associationist aspect of

Yeats's thought, and that the theory of the operation of symbols, whether magical or poetic, relies on the operation of association.

These are all cogent points, but Craig's argument, in my opinion, ends up by misplacing the emphasis. If our associations lead to eternal symbols and images in the Great Mind, then their provisional, tentative, and this-worldly aspect is only one side of the story. Stan Smith makes a closely related point in an extremely perceptive chapter about forgetfulness in Yeats.[10] Forgetfulness is something Yeats often signifies to the reader. For instance, it could be said that his express inability to write the correct elegy for Robert Gregory is a kind of forgetfulness. A more salient example can be found in 'The Tower' (P. 194–200), where, attempting to recall a story he wrote as a young man, he describes how his character Red Hanrahan followed a pack of hounds 'O towards I have forgotten what – enough!'. The deliberate signification of forgetting is part of the attempt to convey the natural movement of mental association. But at the same time it is a reminder of the partial and fragmented character that all narration must possess in the real world of history, as compared with the Neoplatonic world of images and archetypes evoked in Yeats's esoteric theories and frequently alluded to in his poems. As Smith puts it:

> Narrative, then, is a paradoxical dimension. On the one hand, in its very nature, it involves a falling-away from unity of being, the dispersal of the narrated subject into innumerable variants. But...it is possible to regain access to that 'Great Memory' in which the ur-text, the originary myth, is stored.[11]

To look at the question again for its political implications: Yeats's conservatism stresses both the organic character of a society founded on loved associations, and also the eternal verities embodied in a panoply of transcendent images. Indeed, these two aspects are related: what his story of the growth of aristocratic excellence implies is that our associations are formed by those who are learned enough to have insight into eternal beauty and truth. Civilizations such as those of the Renaissance Italian city states come into being when princes have the vision to endow the arts, libraries, and institutions of learning which will instruct and organize the relatively chaotic associations of the people over several generations. The

41

organicist view is recognizable as one side of the contradictory aristocrat identified by Eagleton. Can the other side, the aristocrat as free spirit, really be identified with the Anglo-Irish magus and scholar of occult learning who discovers the images in the Great Mind? They certainly have more kinship with each other than might at first appear, for the magus shades into the visionary poet; and, despite his membership of the Golden Dawn, there had always been an element of individual experiment in Yeats's attitude to occult knowledge. As the extensive occult system which became *A Vision* (first version 1926) was imparted to his wife and him, this isolation became more marked, with evocations of the lonely scholar reading by lamplight in his tower (in 'Ego Dominus Tuus' (*P*. 160–2) and 'The Phases of the Moon' (*P*. 163–7)).

The major contradiction we have been examining can be understood in terms of a central component of Terry Eagleton's thesis in his study of Irish literature, *Heathcliff and the Great Hunger*.[12] One movement in the Anglo-Irish imagination is to seek full identification with Ireland by means of an organicist idea of society. But, as Eagleton points out, the social fracturing of Ireland was so patent that the organicist idea is hard to maintain. In general, this fracturing is the precondition for that semiotic disruption to which Irish literature is so challengingly prone. Yeats's version of this is to set up a poetry in which the contingency of existence in Ireland yearns to approximate to eternal forms revealed by the Anglo-Irish Ascendancy occultist. The next chapter will examine the development of Yeats's occult thought, both in relation to the aesthetic theories with which it is intertwined, and as a natural – if highly unusual – product of the Anglo-Irish tradition.

4

Esoteric Yeats

THE ANTI-SELF

There used to be a tendency to try to play down the importance of Yeats's esoteric beliefs to his writing. Increasingly, however, this is recognized to be an artificial endeavour, in keeping with a reading of 'To Ireland in the Coming Times'. Rightly understood, it can be hard to tell whether the occult or the aesthetic has priority in Yeats's thinking, so profoundly are they intertwined. This becomes clearer from a consideration of the development of his own occult thinking, to which both spiritualism and magic have something to contribute.

The Golden Dawn should not be thought of as a spiritualist organization in the proper sense. It did not involve seances, but rather ritual magic. Yeats had attended seances in the 1890s, but only rarely. However, a series of seances which he attended between 1909 and 1914 was to have a formative effect on the mature development of his thought, and ultimately, combined with influences from Rosicrucianism, magic, and theosophy, was to feed into Yeats's great occult synthesis, *A Vision*. (There are two versions of *A Vision*, one published in 1926 – though it bears the date 1925 – and the other, very different from the first, in 1937.) One qualification is necessary, however: it was automatic writing produced by his wife George which led directly to the system described in that extraordinary work; and, unless we wish publicly to subscribe to the doctrines of spiritualism, we must assume that her own considerable reading in esoteric philosophy, as well as her own powers of imagination and synthesis, had a decisive effect on it.[1]

In 1912, at one of these seances with Mrs Eta Wriedt, Yeats came to the conclusion that a spirit called 'Leo', who had communicated with him before, was in fact 'Leo Africanus' – that is, Al Hassan Ibn-Mohammed al-Wezar Al-Fasi, a fifteenth-century Moor of Spain. As a result of this seance, he began to engage in automatic writing so as to permit 'Leo' to communicate with him. Yeats believed that Arab and Moorish societies had at that time nurtured considerable occult learning: he writes to Leo about 'the Alchemists of Fez' (Morocco). So, in so far as Yeats was inclined to believe in Leo (and there was, as so often with him, a degree of credulity), he could also believe that he had a communicant who was knowledgeable about esoteric matters.

The chief point imparted to Yeats concerned the very reasons why Leo should have made contact in the first place. It emerged that Leo was Yeats's guardian spirit – in Latin a *genius*, in Greek a *daimon* – and that it was in the nature of a guardian spirit to possess a character opposite to that of the being it guarded. To use a word Yeats was to employ in his later writings, Leo was his *anti-self*. This conception was to be developed and refined in the first part of *Per Amica Silentia Lunae* (1917: now collected in *Mythologies*), his two-part exposition of certain essential tenets of his esoteric thinking at the time. In the first part, *Anima Hominis* ('the soul of man') Yeats explores the character and destiny of the human spirit, and, in the second, *Anima Mundi* ('the soul of the world'), he describes the abode, beyond mortal existence, and elsewhere called the Great Memory, of spirits and of archetypal images.

Yeats's first thought is about the antithetical impulse, as he would call it, to escape from what appears to be fated, from the given. As he says, 'When I think of any great poetical writer of the past...I comprehend, if I know the lineaments of his life, that the work is the man's flight from his entire horoscope (M. 328).' It is appropriate that Yeats should think of poets in this connection, for the antithetical impulse, the rage for some difficult ideal not yet within the grasp of the given self, is characteristic of the subjective character, which Yeats sees as pre-eminently the possession of the poet. This helps to explain the way in which a famous epigram from *Anima Hominis* is phrased: 'We make out of the quarrel with others, rhetoric, but of the quarrel with ourselves, poetry' (M. 331). Here, 'the quarrel with ourselves' is an unobtrusive way of describing the relationship of self and anti-self. The tension in this relationship creates the energy out of which great poetry is produced, but the tension is great, for the relationship is as difficult as the very term, anti-self, ought to suggest. It constitutes, so to speak, a discipline of the systematic destruction and conversion of the given self in the light of a realistic appraisal of what that self is: 'The other self, the anti-self or the antithetical self…comes but to those who are no longer deceived, whose passion is reality' (M. 331). And again: 'He is of all things not impossible the most difficult, for that only which comes easily can never be a portion of our being' (M. 332). It is easy to see how this thought is connected with the idea of imitating the image of some admirable person or hero ('In dreams begins responsibility') and Yeats himself makes the connection: 'Some years ago I began to believe that our culture, with its doctrine of sincerity and self-realisation, made us gentle and passive, and that the Middle Ages and the Renaissance were right to found theirs upon the imitation of Christ or of some classic hero' (M. 333). But when he refers to the anti-self as 'he', he is revealing his faith that it is a really existent spirit, and not just a product of the imagination. And before he finishes the essay, he is referring to the anti-self as 'the Daimon' (M. 336). The effort to imitate the anti-self generates 'the mask', as Yeats makes clear (M. 337). Critics are accustomed to speaking of 'the mask' as a highly self-conscious version of the poetic persona, or as something learnt from Yeats's experience as playwright and theatre manager. They do not so frequently make it clear that Yeats believed that the best poets and creative artists were haunted by a spirit (from the imitation of which the mask is formed), nor that that spirit itself has its own volition and is itself seeking its own opposite, 'for man and Daimon feed the hunger in one another's hearts' (M. 335).

THE GREAT MEMORY

The supernatural basis of this conception is expounded in *Anima Mundi*. Yeats there describes how he had come to believe in 'a Great Memory passing on from generation to generation' (M. 345), but had become dissatisfied with this term, because some of the images he encountered 'showed intention and choice'. Hence the term *Anima Mundi*, to denote a realm where dead

45

souls and images mingle: 'all our mental images no less than apparitions...are forms existing in...*Anima Mundi*, and mirrored in our particular vehicle' (*M.* 352). Furthermore, to describe images and apparitions as disembodied can be understood only in relative terms, for not only do 'All souls have a vehicle or body' (*M.* 348) composed of 'animal spirits', but the soul can also 'mould' from animal spirits 'an apparition clothed as if in life' (*M.* 349). Even the 'images' of our 'common thought' are a 'faint materialisation' (*M.* 350). These conceptions, so alien to modern thought, are indispensable to a full understanding of the lines in 'Sailing to Byzantium' (*P.* 193–4), where Yeats asks to be gathered into the 'artifice of eternity' with the sages depicted in the golden mosaic on a church wall. His future status as a dead spirit will not be essentially different from their status as images. Furthermore, when he claims that after death he would like to take a form like that of a golden mechanical bird, this should be well within his capabilities if his imagination is strong enough to 'mould' his spirit to that shape.

Here, as elsewhere, Yeats exhibits that strange materialist bent which owes so much to nineteenth-century spiritualism, with its ectoplasm and photographic experiments. Like nineteenth-century spiritualism, Yeats's occultist thought represents a reaction against materialist orthodoxy which is strongly influenced by what it seeks to oppose. It would, however, be wrong to leave the matter there, for that would not do justice to the radically sign-based elements in the system of *Per Amica*. Beginning to draw together the threads of the two sections, *Anima Hominis* and *Anima Mundi*, Yeats reverts to the topic of the Daimon with these extraordinary words: 'The dead living in their memories are, I am persuaded, the source of all that we call instinct, and it is their love and their desire, all unknowing, that make us drive beyond our reason, or in defiance of our interest it may be...' (*M.* 359). Yeats may be talking about physical 'vehicles' of various kinds, concluding that even the soul had a quasi-material existence. But we then discover that what is often thought to be the essence of animate physical existence, 'instinct', is only the product of our infatuation with, and pursuit of, a spirit from the world of the dead which presents itself to us as a desirable image (and we are reminded that these images themselves pursue us to satisfy their own desires).

A VISION

The ideas to be found in *Per Amica Silentia Lunae* are certainly relevant to the more complicated system in *A Vision* in both of its versions: of especial relevance are the ideas of the Mask and the Daimon. But the further complications are also important to the understanding of Yeats's mature poetry.

The foundation of the system of *A Vision* is a metaphorical use of the idea of the phases of the moon. This use is itself founded in the idea of contraries or antinomies. It might be said that these antinomies are our old acquaintances, 'Grey Truth' and 'dreaming' from 'The Song of the Happy Shepherd'. They are now referred to as objectivity and subjectivity, or, more usually within the pages of *A Vision*, as the *primary* and *antithetical* tinctures, primary being an appropriate term for the given, antithetical for what opposes or rebels against the given. Yeats symbolizes the subjective temperament by the light of the moon and the objective temperament by the dark of the moon. The dark of the moon is understood to be solar rather than lunar in quality. It will readily be seen that here is another version of the cosmic polarities with which we are already familiar. But the fact that the twenty-eight phases are introduced immediately adds complexity. Their chief use is to represent incarnations, for the 'Great Wheel' of the lunar phases is, among other things, a description of the workings of reincarnation. According to this conception, all human beings are born with the qualities of one of the phases of the moon (except that nobody is born into the full – Phase 15 – or the dark – Phase 1 – for perfection of any quality cannot exist on earth). This means that their souls will possess the quantity of moonlight and the quantity of solar light possessed by the phase into which they were born. Thus a person born into a phase near the full moon will possess more of the lunar quality than one born further away, and will therefore be of a more subjective or *antithetical* character. There are many further and quite delicate refinements, but for the student of the poetry the most important one to know about is that of the Mask. Each individual is born with 'Four Faculties': Will, Mask, Creative Mind, and Body of Fate. Of these aspects of the person, reminiscent of the four humours and elements, and of Blake's Four Zoas, the first two represent more or less what they appear to; and the second two represent Reason considered as a creative faculty, and the world that is contemplated by the Reason. The Will receives its character from the phase into which the individual is born: if you are a Phase 14 person, your Will is said to be of Phase 14. But – and this is an interesting point – the other three faculties are said to derive from other phases, and to take some of their characteristics from them. In particular, the Mask derives from the opposite phase: that is, from Phase 28, the phase directly across the Great Wheel. This is an appropriate way of signifying that the Mask is the anti-self, as described in *Per Amica*.

Yeats has a more geometrical method of describing the movements of moonlight and the phases of the moon, and that is by means of his notorious *gyres*. The key to an initial understanding of these is to forget about the shape of the moon itself, and to think instead in terms of changing quantities of moonlight over the period of a lunar month. It is obvious that, at the full moon, the quantity of moonlight will be at its maximum, and that this will diminish in a regular fashion until, at the dark, there is none. Over the same period, the darkness will increase in inverse proportion from nothing to its maximum. Then the whole process will reverse until we are back at the full again. Yeats envisages the quantity of moonlight as a vortex, whirlpool, or gyre of white light. At the full moon we are at the broad end of the gyre. Over fourteen nights we travel to the apex or point, where there is a vanishingly small quantity of moonlight. The dark quality (absence of moonlight) follows the same movement, but in reverse. Therefore, it is possible to depict the regularly varying quantities of moonlight and its absence in terms of two gyres or cones which penetrate each other. The apex of the dark gyre is at the base of the light one, and vice versa; for when the quantity of moonlight is at its maximum the darkness is at its minimum, and vice versa.

The most important consequence of describing the phases by means of gyres is that it becomes possible to describe the movement of history more economically. Like the soul travelling around the Great Wheel, history itself travels through the phases of the moon: to put it another way, each historical period has a different personality, the personality of a particular lunar phase, and history passes through the phases in the correct order. It follows from the initial premiss of the whole system that history is structured around the alternation of subjective and objective qualities. Yeats holds certain socio-political associations with these two tempers. The subjective, or antithetical, quality he associates with aristocracy and the valuing of individual excellence, of the arts and of imagination. The objective or primary quality he associates with objective truth, morality, sincerity, the deference of the individual to the group, and democracy. Not all of the implications of either quality are worked out at once, however. Christianity is essentially primary or objective in impulse (unlike classical paganism, which is antithetical), but, although Yeats believed its long-term effect was to nurture democracy, it has taken nearly two millennia for this to come to fruition.

This leads to an important question: how long is a historical month, so to speak? Or, to put it another way, how long does it take for history to run through all the phases? In one sense the answer is quite complicated, for Yeats believed in gyres within gyres: that is to say, one revolution of a gyre might only be half of the revolution of an even larger gyre. But a simpler view is more useful. An important basic unit consists of 2,000 years. In the space of this time, all the twenty-eight phases will be traversed. Where the idea of gyres within gyres becomes important is that this 2,000 years is itself only one half of a larger pair of gyres. The larger unit is thus 4,000 years. Yeats thought that the period from 2000 BC to the birth of Christ was essentially of the antithetical character, but that the Christian era was essentially primary. This meant that a new antithetical dispensation was about to begin in AD 2000.

This is a conception that is vital to a full understanding of 'The Second Coming' (P. 187). The falcon, turning in 'the widening gyre', is the principle of the Christian era now losing touch with the falconer. 'The ceremony of innocence' – the ritual of Christianity, a religion that puts the innocent child at the heart of its iconography – is 'drowned' in a wave of increasing anarchy and violence. According to Yeats's theories, something like a second coming should indeed be at hand. But it will not be the return of Christ; rather, because of the constant alternation of qualities, it will be the arrival of the new antithetical principle, opposed to the preceding primary principle of

49

Christianity. In social terms this will mean the emergence of an era in which aristocracy is the governing principle, as opposed to the essentially levelling and pacific impulse of Christianity. Hence, 'And what rough beast, its hour come round at last, | Slouches towards Bethlehem to be born?' Of course, a rough beast does not sound like a harbinger of the Medicis – that is, of the kind of civilized aristocracy Yeats claimed to admire. It is not meant to. Yeats thought in terms of centuries and eras, and Nietzsche had taught him that a civilized aristocracy emerged from the tempering of what were originally violent dominant groups. The first movement towards the new era would be when some violent group displayed the ruthlessness and determination to take control in the midst of anarchy. Yeats can be assumed to have had mixed feelings about this (mixed feelings are something of a speciality of a poet who prizes the ability to adopt different points of view), and this appears to be confirmed by the poem printed just after 'The Second Coming', 'A Prayer for my Daughter' (P. 188–90), with its emphasis on beauty and innocence bred out of custom and ceremony. There is a further nicety in 'The Second Coming' which can only be properly appreciated with the help of *A Vision*, and that is to do with the gaze of the 'rough beast', which is said to be 'as blank and pitiless as the sun'. But if this beast represents the initial movement in a new antithetical era, should not it be lunar, and thus have a gaze like the moon? The answer is that it will wear the Mask of the opposing principle: this is absolutely necessary on Yeats's theories. It is thus lunar in character – showing a will to domination – but adopts the Mask of rationality and objectivity. People sometimes anachronistically associate Yeats's beast with fascism, which had not emerged at the time of writing. They are right to the extent that it seems a prescient poem: more prescient than many readers realize.

Strictly speaking, 'second coming' is a misnomer. After all, Yeats's system shows a cyclic alternation of principles, not the victory of one over another. This can be incisively illustrated by considering one of the most important sources of the system. In Robert Fludd's Rosicrucian synthesis we are shown intersecting dark and light triangles divided into twenty-eight segments, and Yeats usually represents his gyres as triangles for the sake of simplicity. The similarity even goes so far as Fludd's mapping historical phases onto the triangles.[2] As in Yeats's system there is a movement out and then a return. But what Fludd shows is the entire movement of time as an emanation from God, followed by a return to God, after which (not long after the second coming) time ceases. Furthermore, the light quality in Fludd's diagrams is solar: the light of the Divine Reason. So what Yeats has done is to invert the implications of orthodox Rosicrucianism: he accords a positive value to the lunar, traditionally a symbol of the sublunary fallen world of mutability, and he also makes mutability the chief principle in the sense that there is no final settlement of the strife or conflict between contraries. To put it in Yeatsian terms, the system is an antithetical interpretation of Rosicrucianism.

If there is no second coming, there is no first one, either. There is only a succession of moments of crisis through which a new dispensation makes itself known. Two thousand years before the advent of Christ, another beast became the symbol of the irruption into history of a new vision – the swan, in whose shape Zeus, according to the myth, raped Leda. This event is the subject of a sonnet ('Leda and the Swan', (P. 214–15)) in *The Tower* (1928). Yeats regarded the rape of Leda as the moment which marked the beginning of the classical era, with its antithetical temper. From the egg of Leda were born Helen of Troy and the twins, Castor and Pollux. Helen was the occasion of the Trojan War; and the twins, in symbolizing division, were also taken to be symbols of conflict. Yeats not only regarded the Trojan War as the founding event of the classical world, but saw in its supposed origins in the beauty of a woman unmistakable signs of the antithetical spirit. Antithetical ages celebrate heroism and conflict in any case, which makes the appearance of the twins appropriate also.

In thus rendering the birth of Christ only one in a series of interventions of the miraculous, Yeats relished a symmetry between Zeus as a swan and the traditional symbolization of the Holy Ghost as a dove at the moment when Mary conceived. He named one of the historical treatises in the second version of *A Vision* (1937) 'Dove or Swan' (*V2* 267–300).

INVERSION

The inverted character of *A Vision* is highly significant. Looked at simply from the viewpoint of literary history, this can be seen in the light of Yeats's knowledge of Blake's *The Marriage of Heaven and Hell*, and of that toying with evil, characteristic of some writers in the 1890s, which itself looked back to Blake, albeit in a way which seems to us replete with misunderstanding. But Yeats's magical beliefs already encompassed the belief that there was value in inversion. His secret Golden Dawn name was *Demon Est Deus Inversus*: 'A Demon is [a] God Inverted.' As far as the Golden Dawn was concerned, this had meant that instead of ascending the direct way up the Tree of Life towards God, one appreciated the contraries 'under the boughs of love and hate' and waited for God to descend towards oneself in the lightning of inspiration. This attitude corresponds to *A Vision*'s preference of subjectivity to objectivity.

But there was another way in which Yeats himself came to think of 'the Inversion' (an occult name for Satan). He was warned by his ghostly instructors that he was too much under the influence of the moon, rather than the sun (of truth), and that he was adopting an 'Evil Persona' (as the script put it) which came from nurturing the Mask by conscious imitation of another, rather than naturally and unconsciously.[3] A different point, but somewhat in the same spirit, was that he was being too deliberate and systematic in his codification of the automatic script: 'dont [sic] deliberately read.' Yeats was unable to act in the spirit of this injunction, but he was remarkably conscious of the abstract and geometrical character of his system. He very often refers to this aspect of *A Vision* and it is relevant that in the first version of the work Yeats can be seen to make the ideas of measure and outline central. He invented a fictional tribe, who in early drafts were called 'Bacleones' and were supposed to live at Fez in the time of Leo Africanus (*V1* 31). But in the published version they are called 'Judwalis', and have moved from Morocco to Mesopotamia. Their name is supposed to mean 'makers of measures, or as we would say, of diagrams' (*VP* 825) and Yeats derives it from the Arabic *jadwal*, meaning 'a stream or canal or mathematical table or diagram'.[4] This mathematical occult science could seem demonic in the sense that the dead outlines of the Tree of Life in his poem 'The Two Trees' were the province of 'the demons'. Or they could seem like something planned by Blake's Urizen, the 'mistaken Demon of Heaven', who spent his time dividing and measuring.

Yeats as the student of abstruse occult science is still the Anglo-Irish mage. As so often, oriental is a disguise for Celtic. And there may even be a Celtic forerunner for the system, in the shape of the early medieval Irish philosopher Eriugena, who expounded a complicated Neoplatonic doctrine of emanation from and return to God in such detail as to include the Great Year in the scheme. Yeats's assertion of Anglo-Irish identity had gone with a sense that the new Ireland could learn much from the wisdom of the Ascendancy, which for him also meant the wisdom of its occultists. This assertion had run in parallel with a self-conscious adoption of a more 'masculine' style and attitudes. *A Vision* is congruent with this position.

This might at first appear a paradoxical claim. Not only is its wisdom oriental and Celtic, but it offers both a tribute to the feminine and a kind of feminine wisdom. Its demonstration of lunar power is, like Madame Blavatsky's *Isis Unveiled*, a compliment to the goddess, whose emblem is the moon. And the automatic writing comes from Mrs Yeats. Now Yeats includes in the first version of *A Vision* the poem now known as 'The Gift of Harun Al-Rashid' (P. 445–50), but then having as its main title 'Desert Geometry'. In this the new bride of a doctor called Kusta ben Luka begins to talk in her sleep – a clear reference to George Yeats's automatic writing: 'A live-long hour | She seemed the learned man and I the child...' (P. 449). The poem goes on to explain that, despite the forbidding aspect of the geometry, the system revealed is an ordering of life: 'All those gyres and cubes and midnight things | Are but a new expression of her body' (P. 450). When woman waxes truly learnèd, she does so mediumistically or somnambulistically. But an important point is that it falls to the male Ascendancy mage to codify and interpret her utterances – or those of the spirits who speak through her. His is the intellectual and analytic part. The artistic parallels Yeats invokes support the above analysis. Speaking of the historical gyres, Yeats says, 'I regard them as stylistic arrangements of experience, comparable to the cubes in the drawing of Wyndham Lewis and to the ovoids in the

53

sculpture of Brancusi' (V2 25). Bearing in mind that he also claims that these stylistic arrangements are of woman's 'body', it is illuminating to reflect that Yeats would have known very well that for Lewis – and indeed for Pound, to whom he addresses a section of the second version of A Vision – Vorticism was quite overtly seen as deriving from a masculine kind of inspiration, opposed to the 'feminine' organicism of the nineteenth century. Yeats's great occult synthesis, then, remains true to the moment in which he turned his back on 'feminine' decadence, and distanced himself from too facile an identification with the feminine rose of Celtic Ireland in favour of a role whereby the Anglo-Irish sorcerer would offer truth, instruction, and chastisement. It was then that he decided to beat woman at her own game of masks and deferral, and A Vision is his most ambitious attempt to do just that.

Gayatri Spivak has some thoughts which make an explicit link between the topic of aggression towards woman and that of deferred meaning in the occult system.[5] The title of a poem which appears in A Vision, 'Ego Dominus Tuus' comes from Dante's La vita nuova. They are the words (Latin for 'I am your lord') spoken by Love in a vision in which Love shows Dante his own bleeding heart and then makes Beatrice eat it. According to Yeats in the poem, this is what inspires Dante's 'hunger', figured in his 'hollow face': Yeats frequently makes the hollow or gaunt face an image of the effects of an overmastering desire. Spivak's point supports Yeats's by demonstrating that the moment in Dante is shown to be an instigation to writing, a writing that, as Spivak observes, can be construed as a war against woman and is full of reminders of 'its inadequacy as a transcription of what happened':[6] the descriptions are deferred and provisional.

Yeats's system could be described as a series of geometrical outlines, the adequacy of which he himself constantly questions. These outlines are themselves outlines of outlines – that is, of the various components of the self, all of which have their subtle bodies composed of animal spirits, or of the components of the soul after death (one of which is called 'the Husk'). The various possible selves, limited to twenty-six of the twenty-eight phases of the moon, are differentially defined in relation to each other, and possess no essence or heart. The source of the fact that all this is so is unclear, and there is a figurative appropriateness in the image of the phases of the moon drifting in a great wheel around a void.

As we have seen, Yeats himself was aware of the stern and chilling aspects of this picture, and of the possibility that his assumption of the role of occult doctor was so deliberate as to partake of evil. A related thought was that he had made a kind of Faustian compact in vowing to study and codify the automatic writing. It is relevant to ponder the fact that, not long before getting married to George Hyde-Lees, Yeats had been refused yet again by Maud Gonne, and had then proposed to her daughter Iseult and been refused also by her. The days immediately after his marriage were marked by profound depression. And then Mrs Yeats started to produce the automatic writing which ultimately issued in *A Vision*. Yeats feared that he might have foresworn passions that were stronger and truer than that which he felt for George Yeats. The speed and alacrity with which he forgot his depression when the automatic writing appeared could seem like the too ready acceptance of the geometrical codification of a woman's body, in exchange for the renunciation of the real body of a woman for whom he nurtured real passion. A heavily disguised representation of these problems is to be found in the play *The Only Jealousy of Emer* (1919), which concerns the events surrounding what is known in saga as 'The Wasting Sickness of Cuchulain'. This play is referred to quite often in the automatic writing.

Cuchulain is comatose after having been tricked into killing his only son. His wife Emer and his young mistress Eithne Inguba wait by his bedside. On the threshold of death, his spirit is encountered by Fand, a woman of the *sidhe*, who is not far from achieving the perfection that is symbolized by the moon's fifteenth night (that is, the full moon of perfect beauty according to *A Vision*). She will achieve this perfection if she joins her spirit with that of a great hero. We understand that, if he accepts her, he will die and join her in the other world. But another immortal intervenes: Fand's enemy, Bricriu of the Sidhe. He tells Emer that he can thwart Fand if Emer will renounce for ever Cuchulain's love. She does so, and Cuchulain lives, resorting immediately to the arms of his beautiful young mistress, Eithne Inguba. There is no reference to the way Yeats regarded his occult system, and he himself never courted a direct comparison with Cuchulain, who was the hero rather than the bard. But Fand makes some reference to Maud Gonne (with whom Yeats had contracted a 'spiritual marriage') and Eithne Inguba to Iseult. The sense of renunciation conveyed by this play, combined with Yeats's fears that he might be courting the geometrical spirit too strongly, makes it less surprising to find that the progress of his later work is to some extent towards the breaking-down and loosening of that spirit of haughty, aristocratic assertiveness which he cultivated in his middle period. In the end, this entails also a new appreciation of the Gaelic tradition.

5

Loosening Masonry

THE TOWER

The Tower is a volume which is steeped in ambivalence towards Ireland, more precisely towards what Ireland was making of itself. Writing to Olivia Shakespear, having had time to ponder the completed volume, he expressed his astonishment at its 'bitterness' and his happy anticipation of a voyage to Italy: the phrase he uses is reminiscent of one that occurs in 'Sailing to Byzantium', the first poem in the book: 'Once out of Irish bitterness I can find some measure of sweetness and light' (*L*. 373). He is bitter and Ireland is bitter. The very emblem of the Tower is suggestive of an ambivalence, one component of which is a bitterness in part derived from the assertive posture of the Ascendancy mage.

One thing to bear in mind is the meaning of Yeats's gesture in buying and then naming the tower then known as Ballylee Castle. People who do not know Ireland especially well do not always realize just how common there a tower castle such as this is. These keeps, originally built by the Normans, were subsequently occupied for the most part by their Norman–Gaelic descendants, who formed an important part of the Gaelic order in the Middle Ages. From the seventeenth century, and even earlier, such castles gradually came into the hands of the Protestant property-owning classes. In occupying a castle, then, and one that is not far from Lady Gregory's Coole Park, Yeats is expressing an affinity both with the Ascendancy and with the Gaelic and Norman–Gaelic aristocracy which it had displaced. A symbolic compromise between these two groups might seem unlikely, but it was increasingly to become a prime example of Yeats's attempts to forge unity out of division.

Renaming Ballylee Castle 'Thoor Ballylee' could be seen as an act of Adamic naming, as some critics have recognized. Better, perhaps, to see it in the light of the quasi-Adamic naming of the Romantic poet. It is, at any rate, a gesture at putting down roots, at possession of the demesne, and one that attempts to look originary in going back to a Gaelic name. In fact, though, in Elizabethan times Ballylee Castle was known as 'Islandmore Castle', which points to the original Gaelic name being 'Caisleán Oileáin Mhóir' ('Castle of the Great Island'). Furthermore, 'Thoor Ballylee' is one of Yeats's 'awkward Irishisms', as R. F. Foster puts it in a different context. It is a uniquely awkward example, though, since 'Thoor' is intended as a transliteration of Irish *túr*, meaning 'tower', but there is not one other single example of Irish dental 't' being signified by 'th' in the whole of the gazetteer. This is an English type of mistake, and double 'o' is the most English-looking of the possible spellings. The effect is of Anglo–Irish compromise yet again: as if Yeats's assertion of his possession of the demesne were saying that he would go back to Gaelic origins, but very much as these could be translated by the Anglo–Irish mage and would-be aristocrat.

Where does the mage come in? In the first place, it is obvious from the poetry that Yeats relished the associations he could make with the idea of a scholar of esoteric learning in his lonely tower, like 'Milton's Platonist...or Shelley's visionary prince' ('The Phases of the Moon', (P. 163)). Secondly, the Tower is a Rosicrucian and Masonic emblem of the created universe, on the pattern of which earthly builders and masons should work. The sense of distant aloofness which these associations impart should not be held separate from those which suggest a specifically Anglo-Irish gesture at unification.

It is important also to consider the immediate historical context of the writing of some of the most important poems in the volume: 'Meditations in Time of Civil War' (P. 200–6) and 'Nineteen Hundred and Nineteen' (P. 206–10) make pondered and deliberate reference to the violent events occurring in Ireland. At the end of the First World War, at the general election of December 1918, Sinn Féin (the separatist and Republican party) won most of the nationalist vote, almost obliterating the old consitutionalist Irish Party, which had once been led by Parnell. Such was the result of the brutal repression of the Easter

Rising. There ensued the War of Independence from early 1919 to July 1921. It is this period that was the first to receive the name of 'The Troubles', and was characterized by guerrilla warfare, ambushes, and assassinations. The Crown forces deployed irregular units, such as the notorious 'Black and Tans', who used ruthless brutality and exacted reprisals, including summary 'executions' and the burning of whole villages. (The behaviour of the British forces in Ireland was profoundly shocking to Yeats, who, despite his past affiliations, could not by this time be said to be prejudiced against them.)

A treaty was signed in December 1921 (ratified in 1922) providing for the establishment of the Irish Free State in twenty-six of the thirty-two counties, and partitioning off six of the nine counties of Ulster to form Northern Ireland, which would remain within the United Kingdom. There were those republicans in Ireland, however, who would never accept the partition, and their descendants are still with us. At the time they instigated the Irish Civil War, which took place between June 1922 and May 1923 – namely, the war of the irredentist elements of the Irish Republican Army against the new army of the Irish Free State. The war was conducted with ferocity, but ended with the defeat of the republican forces.

This is a context that goes a long way towards explaining the word 'bitterness'. It is also a context that makes Yeats's withdrawal into his tower seem both natural and, in a way, paradoxical. The word withdrawal seems appropriate. Not only the associations already outlined, but Yeats's express emotions, support it. This is particularly evident from 'Meditations in Time of Civil War' (*P.* 200–6), which manages a powerful evocation of a mind meditating on the titanic movements of history, on a scale described in *A Vision*, amidst a peace and solitude into which break muffled noises, all the more sinister for that, of a violence too chaotic to be reduced yet to any pattern of gyres:

> We are closed in, and the key is turned
> On our uncertainty; somewhere
> A man is killed, or a house burned,
> Yet no clear fact to be discerned ...

(*P.* 205)

The larger historical context is established by an initial

59

meditation on 'Ancestral Houses' (P. 220–1). Its subject is a Nietzschean question: what if the 'violent bitter man', the powerful aristocrat who 'Called architect and artist in', to 'rear in stone | The sweetness that all longed for night and day', create a peaceful environment in which his children, accustomed to peace, lose 'greatness', so that the effect is to 'take our greatness with our bitterness'. The ironies are achieved silently: those engaged in the civil war have much bitterness, but show no prospect of creating a culture such as Yeats admires. He himself is in part attracted to the tower because, unlike the later style of ancestral house, with its flowering lawns, it still recalls the violence and 'bitterness' of the 'man-at-arms' who founded it ('II. My House', (P. 202)). In accordance with his ambition to be a second founder ('two men have founded here'), he lays out the rudiments of the order he is attempting to make, as indicated by the headings of some of the sections ('My House', 'My Table', 'My Descendants'); yet the events outside render the attempt to make order problematic. At the same time, for all the qualified recognition given to the creative role of violence and bitterness, when forced to contemplate the facts of the civil war Yeats is filled with horror, shame, and sadness.

Powerlessness also. In 'V. The Road at My Door' (P. 204) Yeats goes out and encounters first of all an 'affable Irregular' (an anti-treaty combatant) and then one of his opponents from the new national army, and exchanges talk with them both. Strangely, he then counts the moorhens, to 'silence the envy in my thought': envy that is of those who, not being somehow above the conflict like himself, have a cause they believe worth fighting and dying for. Not that Yeats believes that these particular causes are themselves worth the sacrifice. In the ensuing section ('VI. The Stare's Nest by My Window' (P. 204–5)) he seeks to epitomize the cast of mind which he, having been involved in the movement for Irish national liberation, had shared with the combatants:

> We had fed the heart on fantasies,
> The heart's grown brutal from the fare;
> More substance in our enmities
> Than in our love; O honey-bees,
> Come build in the empty house of the stare.

Yeats's sense of being implicated in hatred and fanaticism also comes through in the final section ('VII. I see Phantoms of Hatred and of the Heart's Fullness and of the Coming Emptiness' (P. 205–6)), and in an unexpected though profoundly significant way. Among the phantoms are a crowd who call for 'vengeance on the murderers of Jacques Molay'. Molay was Grand Master of the Templars, and, as Yeats explains in a note (P. 460–1), the cry was 'said to have been incorporated in the ritual of certain Masonic societies of the eighteenth century, and to have fed class-hatred'. Elizabeth Cullingford has shown how Yeats came across claims that Freemasonry was responsible for the spread of egalitarianism, communism, and class-hatred.[1] Christina Stoddart, who, like him, had been a member of the Golden Dawn, now thought that that Order (since it was masonic) was at the heart of the conspiracy.[2] Her acquaintance, Nesta Webster, implicated the Irish Republican Brotherhood, to which Yeats had also belonged.[3] While Yeats does not seem to have taken these ideas too literally, Cullingford comes to the reasonable conclusion that he is contemplating 'the brutality generated by the idealism of his youth'.[4] With great perception, she proceeds to demonstrate the importance of metaphors derived from building, from 'operative masonry', as she puts it; for Yeats employs the word 'masonry' with some deliberation.[5] On the one hand, masons in the widest sense have built civilization: for instance, the 'ancestral houses' dealt with in the first section. On the other hand, they also appear to be implicated in its undermining by the infection of modern thought: the poem appears to look back nostalgically to the early seventeenth century, when '*Il Penseroso*'s Platonist toiled on' (P. 201), the period when the Rosicrucian temple had not yet been infected by modern materialism and mechanism.

I believe that there is another object of criticism, however, than Yeats's youthful idealism, and that is his middle-aged aloofness, which itself has its political concomitants. After meeting the 'affable Irregular' and the national army lieutenant, Yeats turns back to his chamber 'In the cold snows of a dream'. Again, having contemplated the phantoms of hatred, he turns away and shuts the door, and wryly concludes:

> The abstract joy,
> The half-read wisdom of daemonic images,
> Suffice the ageing man as once the growing boy.

The earlier observation of bees building in the crevices of 'loosening masonry', followed by the ambiguous utterance, 'My wall is loosening', and then by the appeal to the bees to come and build in the 'empty house of the stare', are all suggestions that the aloof assertions of the Anglo-Irish mage, with his 'masculine' style, need to be loosened and less unbending: the Tower has phallic associations, and 'Honey of generation' (that is, of sexual generation: 'Among School Children' (P. 215–17)) feminine ones. This loosening masonry – elsewhere, 'cracked masonry' – is the harbinger of a style and point of view which will claim to be able to encompass the 'feminine'. The 'empty house of the stare' is not just a starling's nest, but figuratively the Tower itself, all strong walls and proud assertiveness, but lacking in 'sweetness' – which is to lack a loving appreciativeness, and thus to be in a sense 'empty'. The Tower is thus another 'husk': a demonic outline, deficient in life, a mask without sufficient spontaneity behind it.

Yeats does not settle in the direction of greater 'sweetness' for some time, however. The first poem in *The Tower*, 'Sailing to Byzantium', sets the tone of bitterness towards Ireland. The famous opening, 'That is no country for old men', refers to Ireland, and the ensuing lines adopt the venerable topos of Ireland's fecundity, here strongly identified with the cycles of nature ('dying generations', 'Whatever is begotten, born, and dies'). In this literary context, the rejection of Ireland gathers force from being the repudiation of a whole tradition. But the grounds of the rejection are explicit: the Irish, caught in the music of nature, neglect 'Monuments of unageing intellect'. We might surmise that, if it is Yeats who refers to these monuments, they will be rather esoteric, and we would be right: they would, in fact, be the forms and images which offer the principles upon which this sensual world is built, principles which will be clear to esoteric philosophers, including those of Byzantium. In Gibbon (whose works Yeats had bought with his Nobel prize money) we read about the survival of Platonism into the Christian Byzantine Empire of Justinian: 'The surviving sect of the Platonists, whom Plato would have blushed to acknowledge, extravagantly mingled a sublime theory with the practice of superstition and magic.'[6]

Far better for an old man beginning his journey away from the world of this nature to sing this Neoplatonic music of Byzantium, a spiritual rather than a bodily music. The address to the 'sages standing in God's holy fire | As in the gold mosaic of a wall' leaves it deliberately ambiguous as to whether the sages are standing there as if in the gold mosaic, or at the same time in the gold mosaic, and this is because of the principle already outlined in respect of *Per Amica*. The images in art also exist in the *Anima Mundi*. This is why Yeats can hope to be gathered in death into 'the artifice of eternity', where, 'Once out of nature', he can take a form like that of a bird made out of gold. Thus he will be able to sing 'Of what is past, or passing, or to come'. That is to say, he will be able to sing of the eternal forms and patterns of things. This is why 'past, or passing, or to come' sounds a little like 'begotten, born, and dies' in the first stanza: the world of nature is patterned on the world of forms in eternity. The poet's future status as a golden bird confirms his escape from the world of merely sensual music. Despite the coherence of this conception, Yeats thought that there might be some room for doubt about the non-natural character of the world of eternity, and in the second Byzantium poem, 'Byzantium' (P. 248–9), in *The Winding Stair and Other Poems* (1933), there is an attempt to emphasize still further the ghostly character of the world of 'images'.

The image of the golden wall in 'Sailing to Byzantium' has a deep resonance in a book that figures Yeats's inheritance of the whole body of Rosicrucian wisdom in the shape of a tower. The golden wall is *Anima Mundi*, an envelope of images surrounding the world, and its hardness combines with the stiff and artificial character of mosaic to emphasize the non-natural character of those images. But in the context of the whole book, the golden wall is also the wall of the tower: the timeless inherited wisdom understood by the Anglo-Irish mage and assertively purveyed to an unappreciative nation.

PROFANE PERFECTION: FROM *THE TOWER* TO *LAST POEMS AND TWO PLAYS*

It is typical of Yeats's method of moving between contraries that, having expressed a desire to escape the pain of ageing by taking comfort in the prospect of turning into a mechanical bird, he should follow on with a poem expressing his heartfelt misery and frustration at ageing. 'The Tower' rages at the indignity of having 'Decrepit age' tied to him 'As to a dog's tail'. But despite the pain of ageing, Yeats's dissatisfaction with the aridity of the stance of the aristocratic mage begins to make itself felt in his work. It is conveyed in three ways, all of which have a tendency to celebrate life, rather than the non-natural forms on which life is patterned. One way is to show that beauty and creative power are most evident where the eternal form is to be found in the spontaneous and organic workings of this life, so that we are unable to distinguish. A second way is to demonstrate the interdependence of the supernatural and the natural. A third is simply to celebrate the physical, especially desire.

The first way is to be found in 'Among School Children' (P. 215–17), where the middle-aged Yeats, inspecting a school for the Free State government, of which for a while he was a Senator, thinks of how Maud Gonne might have looked as a child. Comparing this image with her present hollow-cheeked one, he reflects on the passion evoked by the fine images in whose pursuit or adoration we expend so much energy. 'Both nuns and mothers worship images': the nun, those to be found in the church; the mother, an idealized picture of her child. Yet both types of image can 'break hearts'. The last stanza, however, expresses a preference: better the image at one with some youthful shape of life, than an ideal that encourages life-denial or some learned book of wisdom (perhaps of the kind Yeats shows himself retreating to study in 'Meditations'): 'Labour is blossoming or dancing where | The body is not bruised to pleasure soul.' And he ends with an image of organic form:

> O chestnut tree, great rooted blossomer,
> Are you the leaf, the blossom or the bole?
> O body swayed to music, O brightening glance,
> How can we know the dancer from the dance?

The second way, showing the interdependence of natural and supernatural, is already intimated in a poem such as 'Demon and Beast' (P. 185–7), where demon is the influence of the supernatural, which, for instance, brings mask and anti-self; and where beast is physical existence whose 'instinct' can be awakened only by the images brought by the demon. In *The Tower* this interdependence can be seen in 'Leda and the Swan'. The swan is both beast and, because the god Zeus, also demon. To answer the question at the end of the sonnet, Leda does 'put on his knowledge with his power', for in some sense she must understand the demonic message that a new antithetical era is beginning, and we know she puts on his power, for she is shown to respond to the desire of the beast. As Yeats later puts it, 'Natural and supernatural with the self-same ring are wed' ('Ribh denounces Patrick' (P. 284)).

And finally there is celebration of physical desire for its own sake. Crazy Jane announces in one of the poems given to her voice that 'Love is all | Unsatisfied | That cannot take the whole | Body and soul' (P. 257). But in the same volume, (*The Winding Stair and Other Poems*) a lyric from *A Woman Young and Old* (P. 270–6) goes even further than this: the female speaker avers that once she gave her soul and 'loved in misery'; but, on the other hand, she had 'had great pleasure with a lad | That I loved bodily' ('A Last Confession' (P. 275)). This earthy tendency continues into *Last Poems and Two Plays* (1939), where, in 'The Circus Animals' Desertion' (P. 346–8), Yeats admits that he is going to 'lie down where all the ladders start | In the foul rag and bone shop of the heart'. Rightly understood, this reverses earlier priorities. Yeats had emphasized the images at the top of the ladders in *Anima Mundi*. Now he stresses that those images are emanations of the bestial heart. Lest we should be in any doubt about what this means, the next poem in that volume, 'Politics' (P. 348), describes how the sight of a beautiful young girl distracts him from talk of politics: 'But O that I were young again | And held her in my arms.' This painful honesty of an old man is the last note in the section devoted to poems.

Running in parallel with these tendencies is a new willingness to identify with the female. This is evident in the two series, *Words for Music Perhaps* (in which the wild woman Crazy Jane is given a number of poems) and *A Woman Young and Old*. These two series are both to be found in *The Winding Stair and Other Poems*, the title of which has connotations which are deliberately opposed to those of the earlier volume's *The Tower*. Where that was phallic and assertive, this is supposed to be more internal, ruminative, and marked by sweetness rather than bitterness: it is to be assumed that Yeats held associations with it that he thought of as 'feminine'.

The unbending of Yeats's loftiest pose is accompanied by a new and concomitant willingness to accept the necessary imperfection and brokenness of life. Crazy Jane avers that 'nothing can be sole or whole | That has not been rent' (P. 260). 'Vacillation' (P. 249–53) is a poem that returns to the theme of antinomies: the opening lines are 'Between extremities | Man runs his course'; the second section offers a new handling of the Tree of Life idea, complete with its contraries: sections four and five simply juxtapose two moments – the first a moment of unsought and inexplicable happiness in a London coffee shop; the second a period of gloom in which the beauty of nature brings no solace to depression caused by the poet's remembered follies: 'My conscience or my vanity appalled'. The chief note of the poem is one of acceptance: moments of depression will come sure enough; one should be grateful if life affords one of the other moments, too. In any case, in the spirit of the great lord of Chou, in the sixth section, one may cry 'Let all things pass away', and cry it with joy. This is the spirit also of 'Lapis Lazuli' (P. 294), in which, despite tragedy – or rather, precisely in the spirit of tragedy – 'Hamlet and Lear are gay; | Gaiety transfiguring all that dread.' The oriental note is present here, too, with two Chinamen carved in lapis lazuli, who look down on the 'tragic scene' but whose 'ancient, glittering eyes, are gay'. The note being struck is one of tragic affirmation, a note that Yeats had learned from Nietzsche, but which he fancied he saw paralleled in the joyful detachment, as he saw it, of Chan (or Zen) Buddhism. A more explicit and philosophical statement of this position had been offered in 'A Dialogue of Self and Soul' (P. 234–6): 'I am content to live it all again....Measure the lot; forgive myself the lot!'

With this attitude of mind, the most appropriate form for the work of art is the one that admits the tragic and broken character of life in its very form. It is important that the lapis lazuli, for instance, possesses 'discolouration' and 'accidental crack[s] or dent[s]'. And 'A Bronze Head' (P. 340) – a bust of Maud Gonne in age – merits discussion in terms of the way her whole being, from comely youth to gaunt age, as well as the constant 'wildness' of her spirit, is somehow resumed in a work which superficially shows only the head of an old woman, with all its marks of decay and wastage. And when celebratory, what such works of art celebrate is 'Profane perfection of mankind' ('Under Ben Bulben').

IRELAND: A TRADITION OUT OF BROKENNESS

There is a political correlative of Yeats's acceptance of brokenness and imperfection, and that is a new sense of Irish identity sufficiently strong to permit him to find common cause with the representatives of the Gaelic tradition who had been dispossessed by his own ancestors. This is not a matter of going back to the Iron Age and Cuchulain, but to people who had inhabited castles such as Ballylee until nearly two centuries previously. Thus his poem on 'The Curse of Cromwell' (P. 304–5) contains quotations from the work of a seventeenth-century Gaelic poet, Egan O'Rahilly, who, contemplating the wreck of the Gaelic order, had written with pride about how its tradition stretched back to a time 'before Christ was crucified'. The old beggar in Yeats's poem is modelled upon O'Rahilly, and he keeps faith with 'the swordsmen and the ladies' even though they are all dead: that is to say, like Yeats he believes that the aristocratic order will return, even though now 'money's rant is on'. As for Yeats, he seems to be claiming a kinship between the Anglo-Irish and Gaelic aristocracies, who in historical reality were substantially at odds. This can permit him, in his last will and testament, 'Under Ben Bulben', to incite his descendants, the 'Irish poets' of the future, to sing about the 'lords and ladies gay |That were beaten into the clay | Through seven heroic centuries' – namely, the Gaelic lords and ladies, and the seven centuries since the Normans first landed in Ireland. The Irish tradition is broken, bloody, and tragic. So is life. With this in mind, Yeats, the Anglo-Irish poet, can join hands with the defeated Gaelic bards and aristocracy, and fulfil his early aim of speaking for the whole nation. He need not do this on the grounds of some factitious unity any more, for perfect unity does not exist in the world. Conscious of the future, he believes that any developing Irish culture will pick up the threads of all the Irish traditions, and make some imperfect attempt at unity.

But the Irish tradition, in his estimation, will always be one that has an affinity with aristocracy, and in this way Yeats remains true to a romanticizing impulse born out of the position of his own Anglo-Irish caste when he was a young man.

Notes

CHAPTER 1. INTRODUCTION

1. For 'The Rosy Cross Lyrics', see R. F. Foster, *W. B. Yeats: A Life, i. The Apprentice Mage 1865–1914* (Oxford, 1997), 117.
2. Eugene O'Curry, *Manners and Customs of the Ancient Irish* (3 vols.; Dublin, 1873), ii, 179.
3. P. W. Joyce, *Old Celtic Romances* (London, 1879), 403, n. 3.
4. Douglas Hyde, *A Literary History of Ireland from Earliest Times to the Present Day* (London, 1899), 89.
5. R. F. Foster, 'Protestant Magic: W. B. Yeats and the Spell of Irish History' (Chatterton Lecture, 1989), *Proceedings of the British Academy*, 75 (1989), 260.

CHAPTER 2. EARLY YEATS: THE ROSE OF IRELAND

1. Hugh Kenner, 'The Sacred Book of the Arts' (1955), repr. in J. Unterecker (ed.), *Yeats: A Collection of Critical Essays* (Englewood Cliffs, NJ: Prentice Hall, 1963), 10–22.
2. Hazard Adams, *The Book of Yeats's Poems* (Tallahassee, Fla., 1990).
3. Allan R. Grossman, *Poetic Knowledge in the Early Yeats: A Study of* The Wind among the Reeds (Charlottesville, NC, 1969).

CHAPTER 3. MASK, IMAGE, AND ARISTOCRACY

1. Robin Skelton, *Celtic Contraries* (Syracuse, NY, 1991), 155.
2. R. B. Kershner, 'Yeats/Bakhtin/Orality/Dyslexia', in Leonard Orr (ed.), *Yeats and Postmodernism*, (Syracuse, NY, 1991), 185.
3. Joseph Adams, *Yeats and the Masks of Syntax* (London, 1984), 1.
4. On Yeats's surprise at the role of the Catholic middle class, see David Cairns and Shaun Richards, *Writing Ireland: Colonialism, Nationalism and Culture* (Manchester, 1988), 112–13.
5. Quoted in Carmel Jordan, *A Terrible Beauty: The Easter Rebellion and Yeats's 'Great Tapestry'* (Lewisburg, Pa., 1987) 42.
6. Ibid.

7. Nina Auerbach, *Woman and the Demon: The Life of a Victorian Myth* (Cambridge, Mass., 1982), 23.
8. Terry Eagleton, 'Politics and Sexuality in W. B. Yeats', *Crane Bag*, 9/2 (1985), 139.
9. Cairns Craig, *Yeats, Eliot, Pound and the Politics of Poetry* (London, 1981), 72–111,
10. Stan Smith, 'Porphyry's Cup: Yeats, Forgetfulness and the Narrative Order', in *The Origins of Modernism: Eliot, Pound, Yeats and the Rhetorics of Renewal* (Hemel Hempstead, 1994), 177–206.
11. Ibid. 184.
12. Terry Eagleton, *Heathcliff and the Great Hunger: Studies in Irish Culture* (London, 1995). Contains some valuable discussions of Yeats.

CHAPTER 4. ESOTERIC YEATS

1. Cf. Margaret Mills Harper, 'The Medium as Creator: George Yeats's Role in the Automatic Script', in Richard J. Finneran (ed.), *Yeats: An Annual of Critical and Textual Studies*, 6 (1988), 49–71.
2. Robert Fludd, *Philosophia Sacra et vere Christiana seue Meteorologica Cosmica* (Frankfurt, 1626), 212; *Utriusque Cosmi Maioris scilicet et Minoris Metaphysica, Physica, atque technica Historia* (2 vols.; Oppenheim, 1617–19), II, tractate 1, section 1, p. 45. See Edward Larrissy, *Yeats the Poet: The Measures of Difference* (Hemel Hempstead, 1994), 143–7.
3. George Mills Harper, *The Making of Yeats's A Vision: A Study of the Automatic Script* (2 vols.; London, 1987), i, 10–11.
4. S. B. Bushrui, 'Yeats's Arabic Interests', in A. Jeffares and K. G. W. Cross, (eds.), *In Excited Reverie* (London, 1965), 295, 296–7.
5. Gayatri Chakravorty Spivak, 'Finding Feminist Readings: Dante–Yeats' in Ira Konigsberg (ed.), *American Criticism in the Poststructuralist Age* (Michigan, 1981), 42–65.
6. Ibid. 49–60.

CHAPTER 5. LOOSENING MASONRY

1. Elizabeth Cullingford, 'How Jacques Molay Got up the Tower: Yeats and the Irish Civil War', *ELH* 50 (1983), 767–8.
2. Ibid., p. 767.
3. Ibid., p. 768.
4. Ibid., p. 771.
5. Ibid., p. 772.
6. Edward Gibbon, *The Decline and Fall of the Roman Empire*, (6 vols.; London, 1956), iv. 205.

Select Bibliography

EDITIONS OF WORKS BY W. B. YEATS

Compilations

W. B. Yeats: Selected Writings, ed. Edward Larrissy (The Oxford Authors, General Editor Frank Kermode, Oxford: Oxford University Press, 1997). The only edition which offers, in one volume, ample annotated selections of poetry, plays, criticism, and occult speculation, along with some autobiographical writings, Irish Senate speeches, and letters.

Poetry

The Variorum Edition of the Poems of W. B. Yeats, ed. Peter Allt and Russel K. Alspach (New York: Macmillan, 1957; rev. 1966).

The Poems: A New Edition, ed. Richard J. Finneran (2nd edn.; London: Macmillan, 1991).

The Collected Poems of W. B. Yeats: A New Edition, ed. Richard J. Finneran (London: Macmillan, 1991). Edition the same as the preceding entry, except that it is in paperback and omits uncollected poems and notes on copy-texts. Page numbers for poems discussed here are the same as in preceding entry.

Plays

The Variorum Edition of the Plays of W. B. Yeats, ed. Russel K. Alspach (London: Macmillan, 1966).

Prose

Uncollected Prose by W. B. Yeats, vol. i, ed. John P. Frayne (London: Macmillan, 1970).

Uncollected Prose by W. B. Yeats, vol. ii. ed. John P. Frayne and Colton Johnson (London: Macmillan, 1975).

A Critical Edition of W. B. Yeats's A Vision (1925), ed. George Mills Harper and Walter Kelly Hood (London: Macmillan, 1978).

A Vision (1937; repr. London: Macmillan, 1962).

Autobiographies (London: Macmillan, 1955; repr. 1970).

Mythologies (London: Macmillan, 1959).

Essays and Introductions (London: Macmillan, 1961).

Explorations, ed. Mrs W. B. Yeats (London: Macmillan, 1962).

Memoirs, ed. Denis Donoghue (London; Macmillan, 1972).

Fairy and Folk Tales of Ireland, ed. W. B. Yeats, foreword by Kathleen Raine (London: Pan Books, 1979). First published as *Fairy and Folk Tales of the Irish Peasantry* (London, 1888) and *Irish Fairy Tales* (London, 1892).

Writings on Irish Folklore, Legend and Myth, ed. Robert Welch (Harmondsworth: Penguin, 1993).

Letters

The Collected Letters of W. B. Yeats, i. *1865–1895*, ed. John Kelly and Eric Domville (Oxford: Clarendon Press, 1986).

The Collected Letters of W. B. Yeats, iii. *1901–1904*, ed. John Kelly and Ronald Schuchard (Oxford: Clarendon Press, 1994).

The Letters of W. B. Yeats, ed. Allan Wade (London: Rupert Hart-Davis, 1954).

Other

Edwin Ellis and William Butler Yeats (eds., *The Works of William Blake* (3 vols.; London, 1893).

Biographical and Critical Studies

Adams, Hazard, *The Book of Yeats's Poems* (Tallahassee, Fla.: Florida State University Press, 1990). A thorough application of the principle that one must bear in mind the importance of the placing of poems within volumes, as well as parallels between the placings in adjacent volumes. The author's investigation is informed by a knowledge of both theoretical and scholarly debates.

Adams, Joseph, *Yeats and the Masks of Syntax* (London: Macmillan, 1984). Analyses with some precision the ambiguous or vacillating syntax of Yeats's poetry.

Bloom, Harold, *Yeats* (New York: Oxford University Press, 1970). A complete and detailed account of Yeats's poems, plays, and critical writings, which is not only constantly mindful of the influence of Romantic and Victorian poetry, but also draws precise illumination from the workings of that influence.

Bornstein, George, and Finneran, Richard J., (eds.), *Yeats: An Annual of Critical and Textual Studies, 3. A Special Issue on Yeats and Modern Poetry* (1985).

Brown, Terence, 'Yeats, Joyce and the Irish Critical Debate', in his *Ireland's Literature: Selected Essays* (Mullingar: The Lilliput Press,

1988), 77–90.

Cairns, David, and Richards, Shaun, *Writing Ireland: Colonialism, Nationalism and Culture* (Manchester: Manchester University Press, 1988). A lively and pioneering volume, which, assuming that Ireland was a colonial entity, addresses a range of different types of writing, from the Early Modern period onwards, in which Ireland or Irishness is constructed. There are a number of judicious considerations of Yeats's poems, plays, and critical works.

Craig, Cairns, *Yeats, Eliot, Pound and the Politics of Poetry* (London: Croom Helm, 1981). Includes a very original reading of the political implications of Yeats's poetry, not merely in terms of themes, but in terms of poetic texture and manner. Yeats's provisional and associative style is found to be consonant with an organicist conservatism, and far less notable for its adherence to static images in the Great Mind than is commonly thought.

Cullingford, Elizabeth, 'How Jacques Molay got up the Tower: Yeats and the Irish Civil War', *ELH* 50 (1983), 763–89. Jacques Molay was supposed to be a Grand Master of the Templars, who themselves were supposed to be forebears of the Freemasons. Taking a line about Jacques Molay from the last section of 'Meditations in Time of Civil War', this essay shows how the references to 'masonry' in that poem resound with a degree of remorse and self-accusation on the part of Yeats, on account of his association with the quasi-masonic Order of the Golden Dawn.

———— *Gender and History in Yeats's Love Poetry* (Cambridge: Cambridge University Press, 1993).

———— *Yeats, Ireland and Fascism* (London: Macmillan, 1981). An extremely thorough and scholarly consideration of the question of Yeats's attitude to fascism, which finds that, although he may have been attracted to it for a brief period, the term is simply incapable of encompassing the complexity of Yeats's politics, including the liberalism of his attitude to divorce and censorship, his hatred of brutality, and the long views encouraged by his occult philosophy of history.

Deane, Seamus, 'Yeats and the Idea of Revolution', in his *Celtic Revivals: Essays in Modern Irish Literature, 1880–1980* (London: Faber, 1985), 38–50. Yeats's aesthetic was revolutionary, but his politics were traditionalist.

de Man, Paul, 'Image and Emblem in Yeats', in his *The Rhetoric of Romanticism* (New York: Columbia University Press, 1984), 145–238.

Dougherty, Adelyn, *A Study of Rhythmic Structure in the Verse of William Butler Yeats* (The Hague: Mouton, 1973).

Eagleton, Terry, *Heathcliff and the Great Hunger: Studies in Irish Culture* (London: Verso, 1995), *passim*.

————— 'Politics and Sexuality in W. B. Yeats', *Crane Bag*, 9/2 (1985), 138–42. Discussed above, in the present work, Chapter 3.

Ellmann, Maud, 'Daughters of the Swan', *m/f*, 11 and 12 (1986), 119–62. An essay in the tradition of psychoanalysis, and also influenced by Deconstruction. It is very much alive to the anti-organicist strain in Yeats's writing, as for instance in *Per Amica Silentia Lunae*. It provides a close analysis of 'Leda and the Swan', which seeks to show that fixed gender-positions are undermined.

————— *The Hunger Artists: Starving, Writing and Imprisonment* (London: Virago, 1993), 59–65. Among other things, the place to go for the best and most succinct thoughts about Ireland and anorexia. The pages cited concentrate on Yeats's play *The King's Threshold*.

Ellmann, Richard, *Eminent Domain: Yeats among Wilde, Joyce, Pound, Eliot and Auden* (New York: Oxford University Press, 1970).

————— *Yeats: The Man and the Masks* (2nd edn., Oxford: Oxford University Press, 1979). Still a fine literary biography, though somewhat out of date in some of the detail.

Finneran, Richard J., *Editing Yeats's Poems: A Reconsideration* (London: Macmillan, 1990). A carefully pondered and detailed statement of the rationale of the best possible edition of Yeats's poems.

Foster, John Wilson, 'Yeats and the Easter Rising', in his *Colonial Consequences: Essays in Irish Literature and Culture* (Dublin: Lilliput Press, 1991), 133–48. Examines Yeats's ambivalence in 'Easter 1916'.

Foster, R. F., 'Protestant Magic: W. B. Yeats and the Spell of Irish History' (Chatterton Lecture, 1989), *Proceedings of the British Academy*, 75 (1989), 243–66. A suggestive consideration of the Gothic and occult predilections of the Anglo-Irish.

————— *W. B. Yeats: A Life*, i. *The Apprentice Mage 1865–1914* (Oxford: Oxford University Press, 1997). An immensely thorough, detailed, and wide-ranging biographical consideration of Yeats's activities in the various fields in which he was engaged by one of the foremost historians of modern Ireland. Yeats's activities as magician rightly acquire some predominance, and there is a fair amount of fascinating new material.

Harper, Margaret Mills, 'The Medium as Creator: George Yeats's Role in the Automatic Script', in Richard J. Finneran (ed.) *Yeats: An Annual of Critical and Textual Studies*, 6 (1988), 649–71. The Automatic Script was created by George, not by W. B. Yeats. Her role (and, indeed, her reading) are of at least equal importance with those of her husband.

Innes, C. L., 'Shrill Voices: Yeats's Response to the Easter Rising' and 'Unaccommodated Women: Crazy Jane and Other Women in *The Winding Stair and Other Poems*', in her *Woman and Nation in Irish Society, 1880–1935* (Hemel Hempstead: Harvester Wheatsheaf, 1993),

75–92, 93–108.

Kenner, Hugh, 'The Sacred Book of the Arts' (1955), repr. in J. Unterecker (ed.), *Yeats: A Collection of Critical Essays* (Englewood Cliffs, NJ: Prentice Hall, 1963), 10–22.

Kermode, Frank, *Romantic Image* (London: Routledge & Kegan Paul, 1957).

Kiberd, Declan, 'Childhood and Ireland', 'The National Longing for Form', 'Revolt into Style – Yeatsian Poetics', and 'The Last *Aisling* – A Vision', in his *Inventing Ireland: The Literature of the Modern Nation* (London: Jonathan Cape, 1995), 101–14, 115–29, 305–15, 316–26. These essays are particularly good on Yeats's interactions with the Gaelic tradition.

Kline, Gloria, *The Last Courtly Lover: Yeats and the Idea of Woman* (Cambridge, Mass.: MIT Press, 1983). A Jungian approach which investigates the conjoining of feminine archetypes, especially that of the mother, with Yeats's sense of the tradition of courtly love.

Larrissy, Edward, *Yeats the Poet: The Measures of Difference* (Hemel Hempstead: Harvester Wheatsheaf, 1994). Develops the thesis expounded in the present book (with the addition of a consideration of Yeats's orientalism) at greater length and complexity, and in more detail, mainly in relation to the poetry.

Lloyd, David, 'The Poetics of Politics: Yeats and the Founding of the State', in his *Anomalous States: Irish Writing and the Post-Colonial Moment* (Durham, NC: Duke University Press, 1993), 59–87. The 'troubled tension' of the symbolic status Yeats accords to the Irish insurrectionists.

McCormack, W. J., 'Yeats and the Invention of Tradition' and 'On Purgatory', in his *From Burke to Beckett: Ascendancy, Tradition and Betrayal in Literary History* (Cork: Cork University Press, 1994), 302–40, 341–74. The first essay provides an analysis of great acuity in which Yeats's construction of tradition is shown to be derived from two different and contradictory senses: one, the Anglo-Irish Ascendancy established in the eighteenth century, the other an idea of Irish literary tradition composed with the help of nineteenth-century assumptions.

Miller, J. Hillis, 'Yeats', in his *The Linguistic Moment: From Wordsworth to Stevens* (Princeton, NJ: Princeton University Press, 1985), 316–48.

Orr, Leonard, (ed.), *Yeats and Postmodernism* (Syracuse, NY: Syracuse University Press, 1991). A collection of varying quality.

Parkinson, Thomas, 'Fifty Years of Yeats Criticism (in homage to Richard Ellmann)', (eds.) Richard J. Finneran and Mary FitzGerald *Yeats: An Annual of Critical and Textual Studies*, 9 (1991), 107–115.

Perloff, Marjorie, *Rhyme and Meaning in the Poetry of Yeats* (The Hague: Mouton, 1970).

Pierce, David, *Yeats's Worlds: Ireland, England and the Poetic Imagination* (New Haven, Conn.: Yale University Press, 1995). Detailed, cogent, and lucid study of the relationship between Yeats's works and their contexts.

Saddlemeyer, Ann, 'Poetry of Possession: Yeats and Crazy Jane', in Richard J. Finneran and Mary Fitzgerald (eds.), *Yeats: An Annual of Critical and Textual Studies*, 9 (1991), 136–58.

Said, Edward, 'Yeats and Decolonization', in his *Culture and Imperialism* (London: Chatto & Windus, 1993), 265–88.

Smith, Stan, *W. B. Yeats: A Critical Introduction* (London: Macmillan, 1990). A very fine introduction, which nicely manages a combination of erudition, acuity, and close reading.

————— 'Writing a Will: Yeats's Ancestral Voices', 'Porphyry's Cup: Yeats, Forgetfulness and the Narrative Order', and 'The Living World for Text: Yeats and the Book of the People', in his *The Origins of Modernism: Eliot, Pound, Yeats and the Rhetorics of Renewal* (Hemel Hempstead: Harvester Wheatsheaf, 1994), 152–76, 177–206, 270–34.

Spivak, Gayatri Chakravorty, 'Finding Feminist Readings: Dante–Yeats', in Ira Konigsberg (ed.), *American Criticism in the Poststructuralist Age* (Michigan: Ann Arbor, 1981), 42–65.

Vlasopolos, Anca, 'Gender-Political Aesthetics and the Early and Later Yeats', in Richard J. Finneran and Edward Engelberg (eds.), *Yeats: An Annual of Critical and Textual Studies*, 8. *Yeats From a Comparist Perspective* (1990), 113–25. A reading which is suspicious of the gender-political motives of critics who prefer the 'hardness' of later Yeats.

YEATS AND THE OCCULT

Cullingford, Elizabeth, 'How Jacques Molay got up the Tower' (see previous section).

Foster, R. F., 'Protestant Magic' (see previous section).

Gilbert, R. A. *The Golden Dawn: Twilight of the Magicians* (Wellingborough: Aquarian Press, 1983).

————— *The Magical Mason: Forgotten Hermetic Writings of W. W. Westcott* (Wellingborough: Aquarian Press, 1983). If anyone could be said to have invented the Golden Dawn, it was Westcott.

Harper, George Mills, *Yeats's Golden Dawn* (London: Macmillan, 1974).

————— *The Making of Yeats's* A Vision: *A Study of the Automatic Script* (2 vols.; London: Macmillan, 1987).

Harper, Margaret Mills, 'The Medium as Creator: George Yeats's Role in the Automatic Script' (see previous section).

Howe, Ellic, *The Magicians of the Golden Dawn: A Documentary History of a*

Magical Order, 1887–1923 (London, 1972).

Regardie, Israel, *The Golden Dawn: An Account of the Teaching, Rites and Ceremonies* (4 vols. bound in one; St Paul, Minn.: Llewellyn Publications, 1978).

Waite, A. E., *The Real History of the Rosicrucians* (London: George Redway, 1887). By Yeats's Golden Dawn colleague. See especially the chapter on Robert Fludd.

Westcott, William Wynn, *In Memory of Robert Fludd* (London, 1907).

Index